What reviewers and readers are saying about
The Brandon Roy Story

"Reading Dan Raley write about Brandon Roy is like watching Dwyane Wade throw a floor-length pass to LeBron James. This isn't just a book; it is a breathtaking connection between two greats, an unforgettable assist that results in a rim-rattling finish. Raley is a great storyteller. Roy is an even better story. Read it and leap."

—Bill Plaschke, *LA Times*, ESPN

"This book is a must-read not just for basketball fans, or Brandon Roy fans, but for anyone who wants a candid look behind the curtain at the rise, fall, and shocking resurrection of an NBA All-Star."

—John Canzano, *Portland Oregonian*

"Raley has for many years given readers an insight into sports personalities' lives. Brandon Roy's story is a tale of faith and perseverance. His rise and fall and rise again are the stuff of champions."

—Kevin Calabro, ESPN,
former Seattle Sonics play-by-play broadcaster

"Brandon Roy has proven himself as a great player. Dan Raley has proven himself as a great sportswriter. The combination of these two make for a great story for anyone who loves basketball."

—Bob Houbregs, former Seattle Sonics general manager,
NBA player, and UW player

"Brandon is a great role model for kids. Anyone reading this book will see the hardships that he went through and see that he loves the game."

—James Edwards, NBA player and Seattle native

"It gives me great pleasure to read a book about Brandon Roy, written by Dan Raley—two Seattle icons I know."

—Spencer Haywood, twelve-year NBA player and five-time All-Star

"I want kids to read this book, see who I am, and see that I'm not just a basketball player."

—Brandon Roy, three-time NBA All-Star and Rookie of the Year

THE BRANDON ROY STORY

How a determined Seattle kid became
an NBA superstar and basketball role model

DAN RALEY

Old Seattle Press

This book is dedicated to Nancy, Dani, and Kayla — my home team.

Published by Old Seattle Press
Cover design: Betty Watson
Text design: Stephanie Martindale
Index: Sherrill Carlson
Printer: McNaughton & Gunn
Distributed by Epicenter Press/Aftershocks Media

Cover photos: front cover -- Brandon Roy dribbling, Greg Wahl-Stephens; Brandon Roy in street clothes, Aaron Hewitt; back cover -- Brandon Roy and Brandon Roy Jr., Jim Taylor/ Trail Blazers; Dan Raley author photo, Kayla Raley.

Text photos: All photos appearing in the text of this book are ©2013 Brandon Roy family photos, published with permission, unless otherwise credited: page 184, Brandon Roy as UW player, Kim Grinolds/Dawgman.com; page 185, UW's Brandon Roy and Bobby Jones chest bumping, Kim Grinolds/Dawgman.com; page 186, retired UW jersey banners, courtesy of Bob Houbregs; page 188, Nate Robinson and Brandon Roy, Kim Grinolds/Dawgman. com; page 190, Nate McMillan, Brandon Roy, and Kevin Pritchard, and Brandon Roy and Brandon Jr., courtesy of Jim Taylor/Trail Blazers; page 192, Tiana and Brandon Roy, Greg Wahl-Stephens; page 193, Brandon Roy dribbling, Greg Wahl-Stephens; page 194-195, Brandon Roy dribbling, Greg Wahl-Stephens; page 196, Brandon Roy dribbling, Greg Wahl-Stephens; page 197, Brandon Roy calling a play, Greg Wahl-Stephens; 198-199, Brandon Roy TV interview, Jim Taylor/Trail Blazers; 200-201, Brandon Roy school appearance, Jim Taylor/Trail Blazers; page 202, Brandon Roy as crossing guard, Jim Taylor/Trail Blazers; page 203, Brandon Roy at All-Star Game, Jim Taylor/Trail Blazers; page 204, Patty Mills, Brandon Roy, and LaMarcus Aldridge; Greg Wahl-Stephens; page 205, Brandon Roy and Steve Nash, Greg Wahl-Stephens; page 206, Brandon Roy and Steve Nash, and Brandon Roy and Jared Dudley, Greg Wahl-Stephens; page 207, Brandon Roy and Nate McMillan, Greg Wahl-Stephens; and page 208, Brandon Roy and Marcus Thornton, and Brandon Roy and James Johnson, courtesy of Michael Cristaldi/Timberwolves.

Library of Congress Control Number: 2013930935
ISBN 978-0-615-70101-1
10 9 8 7 6 5 4 3 2 1
Printed in the United States of America

MIX
Paper from
responsible sources
FSC® C011935
www.fsc.org

To order single copies of THE BRANDON ROY STORY, mail $16.95 plus $6 for shipping (WA residents add $2.05 state sales tax) to Epicenter Press, PO Box 82368, Kenmore, WA 98028; call us day or night at 800-950-6663, or visit www.epicenterpress.com.

ACKNOWLEDGEMENTS

Similar to Brandon Roy, this book went from healthy to the disabled list and back, and then changed publishing teams late in the process.

It was written in Atlanta, set to be published in Portland, and made a comeback in Seattle. It went through multiple edits, designs, and a bankruptcy.

A lot of people made this book happen. Foremost, Brandon needs to be singled out for his unwavering support and providing access to his family. Kent Sturgis of Epicenter Press and my first newspaper boss in Fairbanks, Alaska, deserves huge credit for making this book a finished product.

Along the way, the following editors, photographers, lawyers, journalists, NBA employees, and Raley and Roy family members were crucial in keeping this book project going: Michelle Blair, Michael Cristaldi, Andrew Dziedzic, Wayne Floyd, Kim Grinolds, Aaron Hewitt, Kathy Howard, Mike Mahoney, Rich Padden, Mark Palodichuk, Bill Plaschke, Dani Raley, Kayla Raley, Nancy Raley, Nick Rousso, Frances Roy, Jaamela Roy, Craig Russillo, Jon Steinberg, Jim Taylor, Arthur Triche, and Greg Wahl-Stephens.

BRANDON ROY's NUMBERS

Born: July 23, 1984, in San Diego, Calif.
Position: Guard. **Ht:** 6-5, **Wt:** 210
High School: Garfield (Seattle)

University of Washington Huskies

Year	gs/gp	fg/fga	pct	3p/3pa	pct	ft/fta	pct	r	a	b	s	pts	avg
2002-03	2/13	30-60	.500	1-10	.100	18-37	.486	38	13	3	4	79	6.1
2003-04	31/31	144-300	.480	6-27	.222	106-135	.785	164	102	11	37	400	12.9
2004-05	5/26	131-232	.565	7-20	.350	63-85	.741	129	58	26	16	332	12.8
2005-06	33/33	228-449	.508	39-97	.402	171-211	.810	186	135	26	46	666	20.2
Total	71/103	553-1,041	.512	53-154	.344	358-468	.765	517	308	66	103	1,477	14.3

Accolades

2004 — All-Pac-10 honorable mention selection; Pac-10 Player of the Week, March 1

2005 — All-Pac-10 honorable mention selection

2006 — Consensus first-team All-America selection: Associated Press, USBWA, Sporting News, ESPN.com, Scout.com, Collegeinsider.com, and Adolph Rupp; Pac-10 Player of the Year; All-Pac-10 first-team selection; Pac-10 Player of the Week, Feb. 13, 20, 27

2009 — No. 3 retired

Portland Trail Blazers

Year	gs/gp	fg/fga	pct	3p/3pa	pct	ft/fta	pct	r	a	s	b	pts	avg
2006-07	55/75	349-765	.456	55-146	.377	202-241	.838	250	230	67	10	955	16.8
2007-08	74/74	531-1,170	.454	73-215	.340	281-373	.753	348	430	79	16	1,416	19.1
2008-09	78/78	633-1,318	.480	83-220	.377	416-505	.824	370	400	88	22	1,765	22.6
2009-10	65/65	491-1,038	.473	73-221	.330	343-440	.780	285	305	61	16	1,398	21.5
2010-11	23/47	209-523	.400	38-114	.333	117-138	.848	121	129	37	12	573	12.2
Total	295/321	2,213-4,814	.460	322-916	.352	1,359-1,697	.801	1,374	1,494	322	76	6,107	19.2

Accolades

2006 — NBA Draft first-round pick by Minnesota, sixth choice overall

2007 — NBA Rookie of the Year; Western Conference Player of the Week, Dec. 3-9 and Dec. 10-17

2008 — NBA All-Star selection; Western Conference Player of the Week, Nov. 24-Dec. 3

2009 — NBA All-Star selection; All-NBA selection, second team; Western Conference Player of the Week, April 6-12

2010 — NBA All-Star selection; 2010 Western Conference Player of the Week, March 8-14; 2010 All-NBA selection, third team

KEY: gs = games started, gp = games played, fg = field goals, fga = field goals attempted, pct = percentage, 3p = 3-pointers, 3pa = 3-pointers attempted, ft = free throws, fta = free throws attempted, r = rebounds, a = assists, s = steals, b = blocks, pts = points, avg = average

Contents

Introduction

My first memory of Brandon Roy was of him with his chin on his chest. I sat courtside at the Tacoma Dome and watched as this slender young kid missed a last-second free throw under pressure, and his Garfield High School basketball team went on to lose to Foss 54-52 in the state tournament semifinals. I wrote about that deflating moment for the *Seattle Post-Intelligencer*. Brandon was fifteen, a sophomore. To me, he was just another disappointed player in an arena full of them, nothing more, nothing special. We didn't speak that night in 2000 because he and his Garfield teammates were too distraught to meet with reporters right away—they stayed sequestered in their locker room for more than an hour after entering it—and I had an early deadline to meet.

I wouldn't encounter Brandon again for nearly two more years. This time, he was a Garfield High senior with a big reputation, playing in the Martin Luther King Holiday Hoopfest at KeyArena in downtown Seattle, and I caught him coming off a 78-60 victory over neighborhood rival Franklin and superlative guard Aaron Brooks. I interviewed him briefly in a hallway, and remember walking away thinking he was personable enough if not a little cocky. We spoke on the phone a few months later, with Brandon expressing his disappointment over the firing of University of Washington basketball coach Bob Bender, who had recruited him, and I was impressed by how articulate Brandon was addressing a difficult situation.

It wasn't until October 2002 that Brandon and I really got to know each other. He was ineligible to attend Washington, unable to obtain a qualifying Scholastic Aptitude Test score necessary for admission. He was in limbo, left on his own to get his grades in order, work at a shipping-container yard in the morning, and work on his game at night. I asked him for an interview, curious about this solitary existence. Brandon and his dad, Tony, met me one evening during one of his workouts inside Wyckoff Gymnasium at Saint Joseph Church on Seattle's Capitol Hill. A cover story about a young player's struggle and hope emerged in the *Post-Intelligencer*, accompanied by a couple of large photos.

For years afterward, Brandon would mention that story, always emotional when discussing it, always suggesting he was forever in my debt. I didn't set out to do Brandon any favors at the time and didn't require any in return; I was only trying to write a newspaper article about a talented local athlete who, even in his idle time, was still big news in Seattle. The timing of my journalistic interest struck a nerve with him.

"You didn't forget about me when everyone else did," Brandon told me. "I won't forget that."

Over the next four years, Brandon and I regularly sat down for interviews. He was the best player on a talented Washington team even more unique for its openness. Brandon and his teammates were so relaxed and comfortable with their fame they made themselves available almost daily for interviews, which was a reporter's dream. There was a ninety-minute gap or more between classes and practice for most of these players, and they would flop down in the stands at Hec Edmundson Pavilion and talk at length to anyone who approached. Brandon often showed up with a Burger King hamburger, fries, and a drink in hand.

I got to know his family. His parents, Tony and Gina, would approach me after Washington games to say hello. I had known of Tony Roy on a different level. Two decades earlier, I had written about him in the *Post-Intelligencer* when he played basketball for Lincoln and Garfield high schools. Tony and I shared an athletic connection, too; Larry Whitney was Tony's head coach at Lincoln and previously my Roosevelt High assistant coach when I played basketball yet another decade earlier in the city. The Roy family always seemed interested in my take on things regarding the youngest son.

"We were so excited whenever you did a story on me and couldn't wait until the next morning to get the paper and see what you wrote," Brandon said.

Once his college career ended, just a break or two from reaching the Final Four, I figured the kid they called "B-Roy" and I would go our separate ways. Yet I was asked at the last minute that summer by my newspaper to cover the 2006 NBA draft in New York and encouraged to rearrange a vacation trip to Washington, D.C., that my wife and I had planned. I followed Brandon around for two days, watching him get drafted by the Minnesota Timberwolves and then traded to the Portland Trail Blazers a few minutes later, becoming a multimillionaire overnight. Leaving the Big Apple, I figured I was done writing about this guy whom I had seen evolve from a discouraged teenager to a coveted professional basketball player.

Three years would pass, and lot would change for both of us. Brandon became an elite NBA player. I would lose my job at the *Seattle Post-Intelligencer* after twenty-nine years, with the newspaper closing unexpectedly, before working for the *Atlanta Journal-Constitution* and MSN.com. One of my last P-I assignments was to cover a Washington-USC basketball game that brought Brandon back home to have his college number retired. Driving to the arena in the rain that night, I decided to write a book about Brandon Roy. Why not? I had met all of Seattle's unforgettable sports personalities—Ken Griffey Jr., Hugh McElhenny, Steve Largent, Steve Emtman, Lenny Wilkens, and Spencer Haywood, to name a few—and I considered Brandon the most genuine, most likeable high-level athlete I had dealt with. Casually mentioning a book to him on his big night, Brandon smiled and said, "Whatever you want."

Brandon invited me into his home, his parents invited me into theirs, and his grandmother did the same. I called or visited his friends, former coaches, former employers, and former teachers. As a courtesy, I called Brandon's then Los Angeles-based agent, Bob Myers, and he forwarded me to agency attorney Tim Hoy. I fully expected Brandon's representatives to want some sort of control over book content, something nearly every other professional athlete would expect as a tradeoff for personal access, but none was requested. There was good reason. "You won't find any dirt on Brandon," Hoy said before he hung up. That lawyer was right. I looked for something amiss, something regrettable or embarrassing, because almost everybody has something to hide. But I found nothing remotely questionable concerning Brandon's character. Okay, he got into a one-punch fight in high school, and he rarely answers his phone or speedily returns calls, but I learned that he was far more straitlaced than I would have envisioned or guessed.

Roy achieved NBA superstar status with the Trail Blazers before his chronically sore knees put his career in question, sending him into a brief exile in search of a way to return, and then onto the Timberwolves for a comeback attempt in 2012. Throughout this alternately glorious and agonizing basketball journey, Brandon has remained one of the good guys, a hero.

Dan Raley

CHAPTER 1

MODEL NBA CITIZEN

To find Brandon Roy's home in Portland, Oregon, you had to drive down a pair of connecting interstate freeways, up a winding highway, through a narrow side road and into the open countryside. There were enough twists and turns to resemble one of Roy's clever, gear-shifting assaults on the basketball floor. A farm sat opposite his tan-brick Tualatin residence, which was fronted by thick shrubbery and wrought-iron fencing—necessary privacy befitting an NBA All-Star and Rookie of the Year. The front gate of this home displayed two letters in gold against the black metal backdrop that suggested household bliss: *BT*. The *B*, of course, was for Brandon; the *T* for Tiana, Roy's wife, previously his girlfriend since high school, and the mother of his two children.

Three cars were parked in the driveway: Brandon's red Cadillac Escalade, Tiana's black Range Rover, and a black Mercedes coupe the couple shared, though the ever-conservative Roy mentioned offhand that the family might downsize to two vehicles because that's all it needed. A compact, one-rim basketball court was in the backyard, set up next to a sliver of a swimming pool. Toys were scattered everywhere, inside and out. An attentive nanny cared for Roy's two young kids. A couple of lazy dogs roamed the grounds.

Outside of the first-name initials out front, nothing gave that over-the-top *MTV Cribs* feel; nothing was too ostentatious. Everything about Roy's living arrangement, while upscale in appearance and seclusion, was relaxed and comfortable. Similar to the way Roy played for five seasons for the hometown Portland Trail Blazers, his residence displayed an ardent sense of accomplishment, but no inclination to show off. He had fame and fortune, but he maintained an unwavering sense of humility. This residence was a restrained reaction for someone who had won the pro basketball lottery.

"You would never think after seeing us in high school, from where we came from, that you would see us here," Roy said. "People say, 'You're still together.' We both came from families that struggled. We were there for each other. Me and Tiana had a vision. But who would have thought a kid from Garfield High would make over $100 million?"

Tiana Roy once worked for a mortgage company, helping other people secure nice homes. Away from his University of Washington basketball seasons, Roy reported to summer maintenance jobs at a West Seattle ship-container yard near the waterfront and a suburban Bellevue car-rental agency located inside the auto dealership Barrier Motors, to help pay for college. Roy and his best friend, Cole Allen, originally worked near the Barrier front entrance before their sweaty presence made a supervisor uncomfortable and they were asked to move to a back lot and wash the returned Mercedes Benz and Navigator rentals out of sight from the customers. The directive wasn't necessarily racist, more a subtle putdown and reflexive categorization, but it wasn't forgotten by Roy. If only the auto center had another chance to station Roy outside its main entrance and let people see him now, consider the business it might generate.

"We were sitting outside, and we weren't in suits and ties, and our clothes were dirty, and it didn't look good," Roy said of his former job. "Now if I went in there, they'd want me to buy a car."

An inside tour of Roy's airy home, a two-story dwelling built at an elbow-shaped angle, began in a front room disarming for its elite NBA motif. Roy's two All-Star Game jerseys, plus his Rookie Challenge jersey, were framed and hung on his living-room walls. The uniform tops were ultimate souvenirs from a pro-basketball career barely set in motion. These were bright, colorful shirts that signaled success at the highest level for Roy, this man of humble beginnings, and he wanted them front and center in his personal living space.

A replica of his first All-Star Game jersey also hung two hundred miles away in the Hec Edmundson Pavilion office of Lorenzo Romar, Roy's college coach. It was a gold uniform top from the New Orleans game with the following inscription written across the No. 7: "Thanks for everything. Brandon Roy." He did not forget those who helped him reach basketball's highest pinnacle.

Roy's dark cherry office, located off the front entryway, was filled with shelves, cabinets, and overhead spotlights, and doubled as a personal museum with one-of-a-kind memorabilia. He had a pair of autographed basketball shoes from one of his All-Star Game appearances (right shoe signed by the East players, left by the West) and a second gigantic pair of sneakers autographed by Shaquille O'Neal.

On middle shelves were the Eddie Gottlieb Rookie of the Year Trophy, a *Sporting News* Rookie of the Year award, and three NBA Rookie of the Month plaques. He also had three University of Washington basketball plaques positioned nearby, saluting him for, among other things, his defensive ability. A Garfield High School "Top Dog Award" was displayed in a smaller frame, signifying success at every stage of his basketball career.

On the other side of the office, Roy had three more frames filled with multiple photo collections: his triple-double performance against the New York Knicks in 2008, a festive birthday moment, and his college jersey retirement ceremony in January 2009. Another frame held eight neatly arranged pro-basketball trading cards of Roy. He had an autographed photo of his original basketball hero, Michael Jordan, plus Joe Montana and Jerry Rice replica football jerseys, all given to him by a grateful memorabilia dealer after Roy spent an extra two hours over the contracted time at an autograph-signing event.

Roy kept a framed poster of himself dribbling as a Trail Blazers player, tongue out circa Jordan. He had a poster-sized image of Muhammad Ali's face. He was on the cover of *Dime Magazine* preserved in yet another frame. He also had the leather NBA basketball used in his fifty-two-point night against the Phoenix Suns, but with no calligraphy or other markings to signify the personal milestone it provided (his highest-scoring game at any basketball level), which was typical of him; the ball sat anonymously off to the side on a shelf.

Amid all of Roy's treasured keepsakes, the most curious of all was the three-movie *Godfather* DVD box set left sitting by itself, but clearly visible on a middle shelf. The Mafia-themed Hollywood films were his personal favorites, and not just because his mother gave him the collection as a gift. Except for an arsenal of guns and gruff accents, the Corleones and Roys had a lot in common: family and unwavering loyalty meant everything.

The belongings and collectibles, however, don't begin to sum up Brandon Roy. To fully appreciate and understand him, one needed to look past the big numbers marking his often spectacular athletic career—the contract figures and the scoring averages—and consider the overly modest digits that register on his personal life meter:

He is married to the only woman he ever dated, a claim that few men anywhere, let alone an elite professional athlete, can make.

He didn't have his first taste of alcohol until after his rookie NBA season, and even now he limits himself to an occasional glass of dinner wine with his wife.

He has experimented just once with marijuana, in college, and he didn't care for the numbing aftereffects at all.

He has no tattoos covering his well-chiseled body, almost unheard of for an NBA player.

He wears no earrings or glitzy gold jewelry, shunning another widely accepted pro basketball calling card.

He has determined that no matter how much wealth and fame he acquired, there will be zero slip-ups in his interactions with others.

"I'm always conscious of people's feelings, and I get upset when I'm around people who don't care about other people's feelings," Roy said. "I sign an autograph because I remember how it felt for me. I don't want to raise my kids as athletes, doctors or lawyers; I want to raise them as good people. I know millionaires and pro-basketball players, and they're not happy people. I know people who make $60,000 a year, and they're the happiest people in the world, and those are the people I respect.

"You come to my house and I'll be vacuuming in the living room or sweeping in the kitchen. I can never change, no matter how much money I make."

As he explained himself, Brandon diligently sent a text message to his wife, promising to leave a Seattle gym soon following his preparations to join the Minnesota Timberwolves, hurry home, and take control of the kids, enabling her to attend a bachelorette party. Roy acknowledged that a lot of pro athletes, or men with money in general, felt a sense of entitlement when it came to women, that a certain amount of hedonism guided them, and that their egos demanded it. That never has been or would be him.

"It's a power thing, and guys can feel better about themselves when they can sleep with a lot of women," Roy said. "I was a shy kid. I was too shy to talk to girls. I liked Tiana for two months before I ever talked to her. She was younger than me, and I was still too shy to talk to her. Talking to women was never my thing. It was never anything to excite me ... I've always felt good about myself. I don't need anything extra."

Since turning pro, Oklahoma City Thunder forward Kevin Durant has been groomed as the futuristic face of the NBA, someone representing the next generation with his unlimited basketball gifts and a highly marketable image. At twenty-one, he was the NBA's youngest scoring champion ever, averaging 30.1 points per game in 2010. While performing this prodigious feat, he pointed to Brandon Roy, at the time a player in the league just a year longer than him, for giving him personal inspiration.

"I spent All-Star Game weekend with him my rookie year, and the reason we're so close is because he's so laid-back, and that's how I am," said Durant, willingly opening his eyes and pulling off a huge set of headphones prior to a game to discuss an NBA player he claimed he admired more than anyone else. "He's got an $80 million contract and he hasn't changed. He's a family man. That's why I respect him so much."

Growing up, Roy regularly pulled on a Kobe Bryant souvenir jersey and kept close tabs on the basketball player he admired most. He watched the Los Angeles Lakers headliner from an upper-level KeyArena seat in Seattle because that was all he and his friends could afford. Yet, once in the league, Roy drew immediate and lasting respect from this gold-plated player for his ability to hang with him and even show him up at times. Bryant would have surprised no one had he turned up somewhere dressed in a Roy uniform top, so genuine was his mutual appreciation.

"It's a tremendous honor, especially with a player like Brandon," said Bryant, smiling while considering that Roy wore his jersey as a teenager. "He's a great, great player. It makes me feel good, knowing that maybe I was doing something right back then, that a player of his caliber would look up to me."

Compared to the other 449 players employed by the NBA, Roy has no problem presenting himself as markedly different. As for the residual tattoos, jewelry, and braided fashion statements of his peers, Roy doesn't find anything wrong with any of these displays of individualism, nor did he offer any sort of personal indictment of someone else's colorful body art or expensive gems. For some people, especially pro athletes, those things define them, if not provide a road map of their lives. The ink stains can serve as constant reminders of love, struggle, and perseverance. The jewelry-box accessories can be symbols of success and chic. The new-age hairstyle can be a sign of boldness. Yet, while all of that stuff might work for the pro-basketball majority, and even some of his closest friends and relatives back home, it ran contrary to how Roy wanted to be advertised and promoted and judged by others.

Roy has shown he can bounce a basketball as well as anyone while he has maintained an uncluttered personal appearance, spiced up only by the occasional goatee, and that uncomplicated personal life. He has been determined to set his own kind of example, generously reaching out to teammates and opponents alike, as well as fans and even reporters. He won a league award in 2009 for his interview accessibility and respectful demeanor, and wondered aloud at a training-camp practice the following season if he could obtain this etiquette honor once more. For simply being himself, he set himself apart from other players.

"The times I've talked to him he always seems like a great person," Atlanta Hawks center Al Horford said, carefully contemplating Roy while standing in his team locker room. "That's hard to find—someone who's just a great guy. He's someone with strong values. He's someone people want to look up to."

As much as anyone, Roy was responsible for turning a previously troubled Portland basketball franchise—not so affectionately referred to as "the Jail Blazers" after it suffered through one embarrassing arrest after another and alienated a large segment of its fan base—into a bunch of law-abiding and hard-playing choirboys who were admired throughout this under-populated and rustic state, from Cannon Beach to the Columbia Gorge. Portland had no other big-league teams within a three-hour drive for fans to rally around and was located ninety miles or more from the state's two Pacific-10 Conference universities and their popular Division I athletic teams. The city had steadfastly been a clean-cut metropolis that preferred, if not demanded, that its sports heroes present a similar image.

Roy was a perfect fit when he showed up in this slow-paced city intersected by the Columbia and Willamette rivers. Freely mixing in with the community, he made public appearances at high school football games, shopping malls, and countless public events at the team's request. He even served as grand marshal for the city's ultimate summertime gathering, the Rose Festival, which is about as rowdy as it sounds. However, his comfort level clearly came with hanging out in that isolated home in suburbia's open spaces, not some crowded and hormone-driven nightclub in downtown Portland.

He could run with any crowd, but Roy is most comfortable in maintaining unbreakable bonds with his closest friends from Seattle's Garfield High School, Lardel Sims and Cole Allen. He asked them to move down and join him in Portland, to help him transition to living in a different city and maintain some sort of normalcy in his life after becoming an overnight celebrity, a shock to anyone's system. He missed having them around, too. Roy paid for Allen's last two years of college at nearby Portland State University, had him travel with him on some Trail Blazers road trips, and asked him to manage some of his business interests. He had Sims, a licensed hairstylist, move into his home to handle his day-to-day needs, if not provide a personal caretaker to keep an intrusive world at arm's length. They eventually agreed to open up a barbershop together.

"We would do the same thing if he wasn't a professional basketball player, which is sit around and watch movies and laugh," Sims said. "With me and Cole hanging around, it makes it easier for him to be himself, to stay grounded, to stay humble. It's funny how everything works."

In a world quickly transformed to one of hero worship and constant outside interruption, Roy needed his friends to provide a buffer for him. Roy lost all of his everyday privacy after earning All-Star accolades and helping make Portland a playoff team again. Leaving a Trail Blazers practice in his sports utility vehicle one afternoon, a car full of persistent fans followed Roy and Sims for several miles up Interstate 5 as they headed for Seattle. The fans pulled up alongside Roy at seventy miles an hour and did everything they could to draw his attention before dropping back, turning around, and returning to Oregon. Another man intrusively asked Roy to autograph his forehead. At convenience stores, Roy sent Sims inside whenever he had a yearning for something no more complicated than a candy fix, with the underrated Swedish Fish ranking as his favorite simple pleasure.

"I read his fan mail and I can't believe the stuff people feel about him," said Gina Roy, his mother. "I went to church and there was a guy wearing a Roy jersey."

At a time when many high-profile athletes couldn't escape twenty-first-century excesses, from pumping their systems full of performance-enhancing drugs, to frittering away astronomical fortunes on reckless whims, to hanging out with hookers and porn stars, to finding it impossible not to become totally full of themselves, Roy slid into the high-end entertainment world in an open, uncomplicated manner. He had always done things a little differently: from spending hours in solitude as a young kid lining up toy action figures, to limiting his love life to just that one woman, and to playing four years of college basketball, two to three seasons more than most players of his talent level.

When he was a Trail Blazers rookie, Roy admittedly went out and purchased a bracelet, chain, and set of earrings for himself. He thought these things were a wardrobe necessity for the successful professional athlete, momentarily convinced that he needed to follow some sort of accessory guideline. He changed his mind fairly quickly and divested himself of these baubles. Roy handed over the bracelet to his brother, the chain to his wife, and the earrings to his mother as gifts.

"When I first came in, I bought into the hype of the league," Roy said. "I wore the chain once, that's it. Halfway through the season, I thought, 'This isn't me. I'm an NBA player and I did it on my own. I don't need all of that to make me an NBA player. I'm going to do it my way.' "

As for tattoos, Roy never felt compelled to get one, even when his older brother gave into temptation. Allen Iverson influenced a whole generation of basketball players when he entered the NBA with his body under full ink assault, but Roy resisted. He concluded this was a phase that would grow old, with irreversible consequences. He saw people embrace the grid-map look in an accelerated fashion, from a solitary tattoo to suddenly having ten covering one arm. He also saw no recourse for those who regretted this youthful compulsion at a later age. He likened it to a large faction of basketball players wearing headbands again on the collegiate and pro levels, and then not at all. All trends come to an end. Tattoos don't. "You can take a headband off," he pointed out. "You can't take a tattoo off."

Out of curiosity, Roy sampled marijuana just once at the University of Washington, experimenting with something that had been readily available to him since high school but that he previously resisted. "I tried it in college and it wasn't my thing," he said. "I didn't like this downer kind of thing. I never tried it again."

Roy didn't take a sip of alcohol until completing his first pro season, urged on by a couple of college buddies to join them in imbibing. He thinks it was tequila, but he can't be sure. He later tried beer, and was totally unimpressed. "Beer was just disgusting," he said. "I was twenty-two years old and it was, 'I don't ever want to do this again.' Now I better hope I don't get a Budweiser endorsement."

In the NBA, which not too long ago had morphed into a league full of unwanted stereotypes, with players trading punches with fans, players choking coaches, and players generally misbehaving at unprecedented levels, San Antonio Spurs center Tim Duncan and Roy were at the forefront of its credibility revival. They set themselves apart for their ability to merge exceptional athletic skills with impeccable behavior, for being alternately exciting and successful on the floor, while predictable and boring away from it. The only drama in their lives came on the basketball floor.

"There's just two like that in the league: Tim Duncan and Brandon," said Jamal Crawford, a well-traveled NBA guard and Seattle native, who lumped his close friend with the successful and unfailingly stoic San Antonio center. "They're great players, but they're straitlaced, do their business very quietly, no tattoos. Brandon is the Tim Duncan of the guards. Brandon has always handled it well."

Yet Roy and Duncan had a subtle difference. Upon closer inspection, a small ink spot was hidden away on the man who plays the game in south Texas, nothing illegal or immoral, but still a design that effectively made Brandon a person of slightly more moderation.

"They are the exceptions, but Tim has a little tattoo on his back, because you can see it when his jersey comes up," said the Trail Blazers' LaMarcus Aldridge, his religious leanings completely masking his entire left shoulder in a colorful and intricate tattoo. "That's just Brandon's personal preference that he doesn't have one. That shows that he is a strong-willed guy."

Roy bought his Portland-area house midway through the summer of 2009, shortly before negotiating a five-year, $83 million contract extension. He moved from Seattle's southern suburbs to show the Trail Blazers good faith in their long-term investment and reaffirm his commitment to the community. He also moved in order to hand over to his parents the first big home he purchased, a handsome, two-story dwelling in Renton. He put his hardworking mother and father into retirement as they reached their mid-forties, which was his primary wish after obtaining basketball riches. Not unlike his game that he will now share with the Timberwolves, there was an unselfishness that guided his every move.

He wanted to thank his parents for raising him the right way. His father, a former Marine, had shown him firmness. His mother, a one-time school employee, had demonstrated unwavering niceness. He took their best attributes and put them together, and became this unique human being.

"I guess it's just how I see my parents, and it's just my mentality," Roy said. "I never set out to have a good image in basketball. I just wanted to be a good person."

Chapter 2
Roy Roots

Unfold his personal blueprint, and Brandon Roy is the product of a two-parent family environment—a permanent union—something few of his neighborhood peers experienced; stability difficult to find in most urbanized basketball settings. And like everyone else in the sizable Roy clan, Brandon followed the lead of an endearing and stately matriarchal figure, a woman who wielded considerable strength and influence over her universe—Roy's grandmother.

In 1957, Frances Alexander was eighteen and a recent high school graduate when she boarded a Continental bus alone in her hometown of Minden, Louisiana, and rode it all the way to Los Angeles. It took her three days, sleeping as she rode through the night. The bus ticket cost forty-seven dollars and she carried another seven dollars for meals. She borrowed a coat from a male passenger to use as a makeshift blanket and gave it back to him once the bus pulled into the more agreeable Southern California climate.

Alexander had her mother's blessing to go out on her own. She had an aunt on the West Coast waiting to greet her. She wanted something more modern and exciting than her Southern beginnings, where an outhouse was often substituted for indoor plumbing and life always moved in slow motion. This independent black woman settled into her Continental bus seat and waited for her world to change in seventy-two hours.

"I always thought about California like it was heaven," she said. "That was my imagination."

Alexander stayed in Los Angeles for fourteen years; long enough to marry Edward Roy, have five children, and get divorced. The man she called "Eddie" was an Arkansas native and a long-haul truck driver with a sixth-grade education. She was good friends with this man's sister, Ruth, who rented her an apartment and introduced Frances to Eddie. Frances half jokingly said she became better friends with Eddie after they split up.

She lived in south central Los Angeles, in the predominantly black neighborhoods of Compton and Watts. In 1965, she felt the heat of the Watts race riots, which left that part of the city in ruins and the rest of the nation in shock. She lived on East 92nd Street when an overnight traffic stop turned some people crazy and businesses were burned to the ground on East 103rd Street. Over six days, thirty-four people were killed, more than three thousand people were arrested, and nearly a thousand businesses were either destroyed or looted. Three hundred national guardsmen were called in to restore order in the smoldering community. It was enough to make Frances Roy start considering other places to live. In 1971, she moved with her children to Seattle, leaving the heat, natural or pent-up, for a rainy and safer city.

"I wanted a better life for my children," she said. "I wanted a career. I had a sister who lived there."

After attending a Seattle trade school, Frances Roy was hired by Pacific Northwest Bell Telephone Company, now Qwest, as a data-processing clerk. She was offered more schooling by her employer that would have led to greater opportunity, but she declined, urgently needing to work right away and support all those kids in tow. Just the same, she informed Pacific Northwest Bell that she considered herself on the fast track for a job promotion. Within three years, Frances Roy had worked her way into a management position. At home, she was already the boss, ruling with a firm hand and raising Jeff, Kenneth, Joyce, Tony, and Renee. Edward Roy stayed behind in Los Angeles, got remarried, and started another family. "I was the backbone," Frances Roy said. "I was it."

In 1974, Frances Roy bought a white, two-story home with brown trim in Seattle's Beacon Hill neighborhood, a corner residence on 21st Avenue South that would become the family sanctuary. Jefferson Park Municipal Golf Course was located a couple of blocks south of the house, and the equally modest childhood home of PGA Tour golfer Fred Couples was a half-dozen blocks away. College football and basketball coaches stopped there to make their recruiting pitches for her grandsons, Ed and Brandon, and attempted to win her over in the process. Holiday dinners, wedding anniversaries, and birthday parties were hosted there regularly.

This woman's five offspring each left and came back to this home, some with new families in tow, some needing to move back in and save up money before branching out again, everyone always finding great comfort in Frances Roy's sturdy and soothing presence. When her Pacific Northwest Bell job took her to suburban Bellevue, she rented an apartment to avoid the interminable commute over the congested State Route 520 floating bridge. She hung onto her Beacon Hill house, temporarily turning it over to her children, because no one wanted to part with it; its very existence in the family was a source of great comfort.

Frances Roy attended her children's sporting events, and then her grandchildren's games, always making sure these outings were treated as gatherings to be shared by the entire family. She compiled three scrapbooks full of everyone's newspaper clippings and photographs that she stored in her basement. She collected their trophies and awards and put them in her hope chest. Back then, the kids' recreation league basketball games were looked at as something for the Roys to celebrate together in an all-inclusive manner, and hardly as the springboard for the NBA draft and a lifetime of fame and riches for one of their own.

"It never crossed my mind that Brandon would be out there doing all those things he's doing now," Frances Roy said earnestly. "It's hard for me to see him as anything but Brandon, not a celebrity. People say, 'Do you know Brandon Roy?' and I say, 'Yes, that would be my grandson.' They just go overboard, even at the doctor's office. I don't see him as this idol for other folks."

"I just went to see my nephews play," said Renee Roy, Brandon's aunt and a Metro bus driver. "I never knew much about anyone going to the pros. I didn't know what a draft was."

Frances and Eddie Roy's fourth child, Edward Anthony Roy, better known as Tony, was a basketball player, and fancied himself a good one. As grade-schoolers, he and his brothers visited their remarried father in Los Angeles and spent summer days in pickup games in different community-center gyms. They used this exposure to advanced California competition to return to Seattle as better players and successfully move through the different layers of Northwest basketball.

As a junior at Seattle's Lincoln High School, Tony was a guard and one of the headliners for a team nicknamed the Lynx. He was coached by Larry Whitney, a Lincoln alumnus, former player, and emotional leader. Roy thrived at this school playing for this man. Yet as a senior, he was forced to find a new place to play when Lincoln and Queen Anne, both centrally located high schools in the city and rich in athletic tradition, were closed because of steady drops in citywide enrollment. He transferred to the basketball powerhouse, Garfield, thinking he could compete with anyone. He didn't make a smooth transition.

Whenever this Roy suited up for the Bulldogs, a sign was held high in the crowd: *Start Tony*. Before each game during the 1981-82 basketball season, as the players walked to the middle of the floor for the opening tipoff, Gina Crawford stood in the stands of Garfield's aging and often crowded gym in Seattle's Central Area and waved her homemade placard with the personalized message. She wasn't happy that Tony Roy, her boyfriend of three years, was relegated to the bench. She felt he deserved better. He wasn't too thrilled with his substitute's role, either. He had been a Lincoln starter, a proven star. At every game, the constant reminder came from that solitary presence in the bleachers: *Start Tony*.

Yet while Gina Crawford's protest methods were admirable, the results most likely were negligible. It's possible everyone spotted her handiwork on game day except the person for whom it was intended.

"There was always so much going on there, I may have never seen that sign," suggested Garfield coach Al Hairston, who briefly was a Seattle

SuperSonics guard and spent a majority of his own NBA career watching the opening tip from the far end of the bench. "Garfield was kind of a tough nut to crack. We had a system in place. For a guy from the outside to break into the starting lineup was tough."

The situation facing the cerebral Hairston with this particular Garfield team was a challenging one. He had perhaps ten players on the roster who were capable of starting for him. This former professional athlete, who two years earlier had directed the Bulldogs to a 25-0 record and state championship in his first season as head coach, chose his starters from an impressive nucleus of returning veterans. One of them was six-foot-nine center Van Beard, who later accepted a basketball scholarship from the University of Arizona and its new coach at the time, Lute Olson, someone who would revisit Garfield more than two decades later and try to recruit another Bulldogs player, one named Roy. Mix in a couple of highly competitive transfers in Jerry Travis and Tony Roy, both starters from that discontinued Lincoln High program, and the Bulldogs had a personnel logjam.

"To even make that Garfield team, you had to be a pretty good player," Hairston pointed out.

Tony Roy was a six-foot guard who possessed exemplary ball-handling ability and could score in bunches. He played a lot of minutes for this coach. He just didn't start when the season opened. He didn't start when it reached its halfway point. And he wasn't starting when it was headed for the stretch run and postseason. Gina Crawford wasn't interested in excuses. Before making her sign, she put together a petition, brought it to the gym, and passed it around to Garfield basketball fans, requesting signatures that supported the same dogged cause: Start Tony. Yet Hairston said he never saw any of this campaign paperwork, either. In the end, the situation sorted itself out on its own.

Favored to capture the Metro League championship and advance to the 3A boys' state tournament, which was a winter rite of passion for Garfield, this deep Bulldogs team didn't mesh and failed to meet expectations. Disgruntled players dropped off or were thrown off the team as Garfield slumped to a 15-9 record, finished as the league runner-up, and missed out on the state tournament. "I never got a Metro title," mused Tony Roy, whose Lincoln team placed second in its division the year before. "I was always a bridesmaid."

Yet there was a positive development among all of the Bulldogs' late-season discontent and roster turnover. Crawford finally received her wish and all of that unwavering loyalty was rewarded. Roy started the final three games of the Metro season, broke loose for a career-best twenty-six points against Chief Sealth High School, and was even named all-conference honorable mention after playing mostly as a substitute.

This is how Brandon Roy, born to these deeply committed high-school sweethearts two years after their graduation, received his exquisite basketball genes. They came wrapped in a well-rounded package, imported from both Mars and Venus, in part explaining the Roy versatility that would be envied across the game's top tier. His basketball skills had a deep-rooted connection to Garfield, which was his destination as well. His front-and-center father, Tony, taught him a basic skill set, if not everlasting patience and competitiveness. His effervescent mother, Gina, gave him the gift of passion and relentless persistence.

Tony Roy and Gina Crawford first met in the eighth grade at Hamilton Middle School in north Seattle, with both bused across town. They regularly talked on the phone. After a year apart at different schools as ninth-graders, they were reunited at Lincoln High School as sophomores and became inseparable. "She held my hand, so I figured we had become boyfriend and girlfriend," Tony Roy said. After graduating from Garfield, life turned a little chaotic for this young couple, but they made it work. Their oldest son, Edward Anthony Roy II, was born at the end of that first post-high-school summer.

An unmarried teenage father with family responsibilities, Tony Roy signed up for a three-year stint in the U.S. Marine Corps. This required boot-camp training in California, advanced training in Alabama, active duty at San Diego's Camp Pendleton, and a year of service overseas in Okinawa, Japan. He needed to grow up quick and find a career, and he decided this was the best way to get started. He was drawn to the Marines and the demanding lifestyle that produced robust men whom he so wanted to emulate.

"When Ed was born that August, I knew I had to get a job," he said. "My brother suggested the Air Force, but I looked into the other branches. The Marine Corps had young guys who were strong and athletic."

Tony Roy was promoted to the rank of Lance Corporal E5, even with the family's "five-star general" stationed back home making it clear she would have preferred that he pursue a much different direction in life.

"My hope was Tony would go to school," Frances Roy said. "That was my plan. I didn't want him in the Marines."

Well into this military commitment and parenthood, Tony and Gina Roy were married in Los Angeles on November 19, 1983. There were people who nearly prevented this from happening without knowing it. An impending Greyhound bus strike turned a two-hour ride from Camp Pendleton into an agonizing six-hour ordeal for the groom, with strike supporters purposely driving slowly in front of his southbound coach, trying to stop it and the military man inside from reaching the next destination.

The Roys paid seventy-five dollars to get married, plus an extra ten dollars to reopen the chapel because they arrived late. Gina's brother was their witness. The typical engagement-marriage sequence was done in stages because of family economics. Two months later, Gina Roy, who temporarily returned to Seattle, received her wedding ring in the mail from Tony.

Their first home was an apartment in Oceanside, California, north of San Diego, which was all they could afford on his entry-level military salary. The place was nice enough, though the amenities needed a serious upgrade. They kept a television, perched on a crate, which offered just one channel predominantly showing San Diego Padres games. Gina Roy became a baseball fan.

On July 23, 1984, a second son, Brandon Dawayne Roy, was born at Naval Hospital Camp Pendleton in San Diego. Again there were unforeseen challenges to an important family milestone, similar to the wedding. With the Olympic Games unfolding in Los Angeles the following month and its trappings spilling all over Southern California, Gina Roy, in full labor, had to wait for a runner carrying the ceremonial torch, and all the security and spectators that came with it, to pass through the base before she could be transported to the military hospital. NBA-bound Brandon Roy hadn't been delivered yet, but in all of his final kicking and pushing to get out of his mother's womb he almost drew his first five-second call for failing to land inbounds in the amount of time required.

All the same, when Roy emerged into the world for the first time, he didn't make a sound. The delivery-room doctor twice rapped him on the bottom to spur a response, but he remained stoic and silent, to the extent that the physician had to look twice to make sure the newborn was alive and breathing. It was a serious demeanor that hasn't changed much.

While the first Roy son was named after his dad, this second one's christening resulted from a little more creativity, if not impulsiveness. On earlier trips from Seattle to visit her Marine Corps husband, Gina Roy always stayed with her brother and sister-in-law, who operated a child day-care center in Inglewood, California. Gina watched as a fun-loving Russian woman came for her son and each day energetically called out, "Where's my baby babushka?" This was just a nickname. Gina Roy was told that the child's real name was Brandon. She was so smitten by this heavily accented woman's coddling of her boy, and the different names involved, and the passion involved, she came away with inspiration for her second son's name. "Brandon is named after a Russian baby," Gina Roy said.

Once his Marine obligation was fulfilled overseas, Tony Roy rejoined his family in Seattle. He applied for unemployment and medical benefits that were due him. He also had a tough time finding a regular job. He was lying in bed one morning at the family home on Beacon Hill when his mother, demonstrating her resourcefulness and determination, drove up, impatiently honked the car horn, got out, and announced to him, "We're going to get a job today. Put your clothes on." Frances Roy escorted her son to several government-sponsored employers across the city, such as the U.S. Postal Service and Metro Transit. He filled out applications and wanted to hide. "People were laughing at me, walking in with my mom," Tony Roy said.

Metro hired him as a driver, originally part-time, leading to a seventeen-year career. Tony Roy worked all over the city and moved from regular buses to electric coaches. He had just one minor accident in all that time, when a distracted Hawaiian tourist in a rental car suddenly veered in front of his bus; a few dents were the result. He worked at night and slept during the day, which required his young boys, Ed and Brandon, to be quiet when they were home, with Gina Roy regularly serving the boys gentle reminders.

A daughter, Jaamela, three years younger than Brandon, was added to the Roy family roster in 1987. She was personable and enjoyed people showing her attention. Her earliest years were spent riding Metro around the city. The three Roy kids often finished dad's bus shifts with him. Jaamela Roy provided entertainment on some of these late-night excursions as they wove their way back to the bus barn.

"They would meet me at the end of the line and ride into town with me, especially Jaamela," Tony Roy said. "I'd let her sing into the microphone if nobody else was on board."

This was a family of modest means that never missed out on much. Tony Roy pulled plenty of overtime shifts to assure that. The Roys were fiercely protective of each other. It could get comical at times. Gina Roy took jobs as a lunchroom attendant at a couple of south-end schools and left a positive impression on everyone she encountered. She was so friendly and gregarious that some of the students felt compelled to holler out to her wherever they spotted her away from work. Someone would recognize her at the grocery store or a restaurant and want her full attention. Many of these students had a pet name for her, one that would infuriate a young Brandon Roy to no end. He would grow up trying to please everyone, but not when it came to sharing the women in his life.

"Some kids called her 'Mom,' " Tony Roy said. "Brandon used to hate it. He used to tell me, 'That's not their mom, that's my mom.' "

Brandon Roy was equally protective of his grandmother. In 1990, Frances Roy retired from her telephone company job after accepting a buyout offer. She needed a cane to get around. Relatives and friends surrounded her at all times on Beacon Hill, seeking her approval and counsel. She remained the calming influence in everyone's sometimes complicated lives. In the background, her TV set often was tuned to CNN, keeping her in touch with an ever-changing and hero-worshipping culture that counts her grandson among its targeted and dissected individuals.

A solitary photo of Brandon Roy in a Trail Blazers uniform was displayed on her mantle, but little else in her living room to suggest that Frances Roy was related to one of the NBA's most talented and well-paid players. She shrugged at any mention of his personal wealth, not interested in sharing any of it, more wishful that it didn't corrupt anyone. She insisted Brandon was no different than the rest of her family members who turned out polite and hardworking at her insistence. As one of her fifteen grandchildren, he received the same marching orders as his parents, aunts and uncles, and all those cousins who came before and after him.

If his grandmother gave Brandon Roy any special gift that only the two of them share, it was this: behind their reserved and relaxed manner was an impish character with a quick wit deep down, one likely to spring out at any time and leave people amused and laughing.

"I believe it's a Roy thing that he's very humble, but all of my kids are that way," Frances Roy said. "We're a very close-knit family. I just told them, 'I want you kids to do well for yourself. I want you to take care of yourself. I don't want you to take care of me. God will do that. Just stay out of my pocket.' "

CHAPTER 3

DELRIDGE DAYS

There was nothing remarkable at all about the ground-floor residence at 4137 Delridge Way Southwest, outside of the fact that Brandon Roy was raised there, and he called this place home longer than any other. The boxlike, gray house was located on the east side of West Seattle and contained three rental units—a living arrangement not unusual for a section of the city patched together with multifamily dwellings.

The top floor, main floor, and basement occupants each had a mailbox out front and a different address. The front lawn was nothing more than a short, narrow strip of weeds surrounded by concrete on all sides. The backyard consisted of cement and dirt. Landscaping was a solitary bush planted near a stairway and a telephone pole stationed at the curb that held up a sign calling for *No Parking, 4-6 p.m.* Signs posted on the exterior of the home contradicted each other: *No Trespassing* and *For Rent*. Similar to a Boston or Philadelphia row house, this place was crammed into the middle of a block filled with look-alike structures and limited privacy. It practically sat on top of the busy four-lane street that passed in front of it, which made it impossible for those inside to escape the inner-city din.

From 1993 to 2006, the aspiring pro-basketball player and his family squeezed into these cozy quarters, which consisted of three bedrooms and a solitary bathroom. They previously lived briefly at Frances Roy's centralized Beacon Hill house, in SeaTac near the airport, and at yet another West Seattle location, but this was where the kids were raised and memories were made. The Roys were the first renters to move into this split-level home, the newness of it all making everyone nearly as excited as if the place had been purchased. The main floor filled their basic needs, but not surprisingly, this housing situation also made its most-famous occupant yearn for something bigger and better.

"We stayed in apartments my whole life," Brandon Roy said. "I always wanted to get a house with grass."

Delridge Way cut through one of the more diverse sections of Seattle. Women waited at bus stops dressed in African-styled clothing. Men drove taxis wearing turbans and long beards. Immigrants from all parts of the globe lived and worked side by side. Yet ethnicity played only a partial role in creating a well-stirred urban mix. Two blocks north of the rental home were entrance and exit ramps connected to the high-arching West Seattle bridge. Completed the same year Brandon Roy was born as a replacement for the original and damaged overpass, the bridge separated the spacious waterfront area, filled with orange container cranes and deep-water docks, from a community harboring residential, industrial, and social services buildings.

Between the house and the bridge was the Department of Social and Health Services (DSHS) in a distinctive-looking building composed of almost all plate-glass windows. DSHS took up considerable space across the street from the rusted, steaming Nucor Steel plant. Families and metals were welded together at these respective facilities. Both had oversized American flags prominently on display, whipping in the breeze coming off nearby Elliott Bay. A half-block south of the house was the block-long Delridge Playfield, which offered a community center, youth and family services center, and a park area full of baseball diamonds, soccer, and football fields, and swing sets. A half-dozen blocks south was South Seattle Community College. A full schedule of games and classes kept Delridge Way traffic always on the heavy side.

The Roys moved into this crowded neighborhood because it was accessible and affordable. It also brought extended family members together. An aunt lived on the same side of the street. Another aunt lived across the street. It was a tight squeeze inside the Roys' Delridge Way home, but it felt safe. Kids' imaginations ran wild there, with Brandon leading this youthful fast break. He made up all sorts of games for the others to play. They shot at the refrigerator with toy guns, as if the kitchen appliance were some sort of huge robot bearing down on them. They played *Mission Impossible*, with Brandon always leading them on some sort of dangerous assignment.

"He would have us like we were in a movie," said Jaamela Roy, Roy's sister. "It would be so much fun."

When he wasn't immersed in this make-believe world, Brandon would lose himself in another. For hours, he would play alone inside the house with his action figures while other kids ran around outside. There were all kinds of toy men in his collection of playthings, including Army soldiers and X-Men. He lined them up in different formations. He lined them up on a dining-room table. He lined them up under the table. He once dismantled the unused bottom half of a bunk bed, hauling the mattress off to storage, so he could have plenty of room to play with these toys.

"Every other kid would be out playing and he'd be under the table with his men, anywhere he could put them out," said Eddie Jamison, a longtime friend of Brandon's grandmother and the Roy family. "I was getting a little worried about him playing with the men all the time."

There was an early period of his life when Brandon Roy had to balance a long day of school and team practice that involved any number of sporting endeavors. By nightfall, his mother wanted everyone to get home, take a bath, and climb into bed. Young Brandon had another idea. He wanted an extra forty-five minutes for himself. He needed this time alone to play with his action figures and lobbied hard for it. His wish was granted because of his persistence.

"He was negotiating contracts way before it was time," Gina Roy pointed out.

As an elementary-school student, Brandon Roy gathered up cardboard, paper, and discarded toilet-paper rolls and cut and twisted and taped them into intricate settings. He built coliseums. He made gymnasiums. He drew intricate details on all of these homemade creations. He gave his precious action figures a battleground or a playground. Roy also gave one of his toy men a burial. He owned a Spider-man figure that wore out from overuse.

The arms and legs fell off. He taped them back on until the pieces would no longer stay together. He finally relented and gave up on this toy. He scrounged up a little box, dug a deep hole in the backyard, and put his plastic superhero to rest.

When he wasn't so solemn, Brandon Roy was a subtle prankster. When his mother napped, he often was lifted onto the counter by his brother Ed and in tandem they snuck cookies. Brandon liked to make his siblings laugh or cringe. He mixed together concoctions of syrup, water, flour, and whatever he could get his hands on, and told his older brother it was chocolate milk, impishly encouraging him to drink it. Ed learned fairly soon to pass on these refreshment offers. Brandon also took great pleasure in Ed's serious fear of snakes, and he once left a rubberized yet realistic-looking reptile to greet his sibling outside the shower, and then waited for the shrieks that inevitably came. He took great joy in hiding in a darkened room and jumping out and scaring the others, especially his mother. He loved having the upper hand in snowball fights, too.

"Brandon was one of those kids you had to keep an eye on," Ed Roy said. "If you didn't, he was plotting. I wanted to break his neck sometimes."

"We have so many memories; memories where I wanted to choke him," Jaamela Roy said.

Tony Roy owned a pair of clippers and used to dole out the family haircuts. He preferred that his boys keep their hair short and neat, not a surprising demand from a former Marine. Tony Roy wasn't pleased the day he came home from work and found that Ed had taken the clippers and eagerly tried his hand at grooming his six-year-old brother.

"We got in trouble with Dad," Brandon Roy recalled. "There were big patches, big holes, in my hair."

Ed Roy offered a far different version than his brother: "I remember Brandon putting big patches in our little cousin's hair."

Basketball entered their lives when they were in grade school, but initially as just one of their many activities. As young kids, the Roy brothers started with an eight-foot hoop nailed to the side of the house, then briefly had two basketball hoops in operation on different sides of the crowded housing complex. One basket was positioned near the garage in back, the other located closer to the street. They downsized to the more secluded basket after balls continually bounced into the street, causing drivers to swerve dangerously and angrily honk their horns. They lowered the rims and held dunk contests. The rims repeatedly were bent and broken when the siblings reached their teenage years and started playing a more airborne game. Their hoop games took on all forms. Brandon's sister was not exempt from the driveway challenges, either. These siblings went at it practically the moment they stepped off the bus together.

"We would talk all day at school, that we were going to go at it when we got to the house," Jaamela Roy recounted. "I'd have my skirt on and shoes off and we'd play in the driveway."

Yet another Delridge neighbor had his own NBA ambitions. Terrence Williams, later a New Jersey Nets, Houston Rockets, and Sacramento Kings guard who attended Seattle's Garfield and Rainier Beach high schools before playing collegiately at Louisville, lived in an apartment across the street. Williams was a constant fixture at the Roys' household, eager to take part in their daily pickup basketball games and highly dependent on them to provide an alternative place to hang out.

Williams was twelve when he notice Brandon Roy, three years older, shooting baskets across the street. He asked if he could play alongside him. An accommodating Roy gave him some pointers on how to use the backboard on certain shots, which only encouraged his young protégé to want more. Williams knocked on the door practically every day thereafter, often locked out of his home, but a conscientious basketball student just the same.

"He learned how to play basketball in my driveway," Tony Roy said. "I like to think his formative years came in my driveway."

A common sight at the Delridge Way house was the Roy family pulling away from it. Everyone piled into a 1987 burgundy Ford Aerostar van and traveled across town to Rainier Playfield or some south-end gymnasium for kids' practices in just about any sport. They were gone for hours. The unused middle row of seats in the van was pulled out to make it easier for kids to do homework, sleep, eat, or just hang out while waiting for the end of practice, and then they went home.

"One of the things I really respected about my parents is we didn't have all of the things, but we had some things," said Ed Roy, who walked away from a place he simply referred to as "4137" with only good memories. "The one thing you could say about it was it was our house."

Before becoming teenagers, the Roy brothers didn't need much else to entertain them. If they weren't in the gym or on a field, they were comfortable lounging around their home. When Brandon wasn't sidetracked by his action figures or dreaming up pranks, the siblings watched movies or played laser tag, engaging in innocent kid stuff. They preferred to hang out at the house rather than roam the neighboring streets, which sometimes echoed with late-night gunfire, brought police sirens screaming up Delridge Way, and warranted mention on the TV news with an occasional casualty. The Roys loosely referred to those who hung out at the park as "community center kids." They were self-proclaimed homebodies.

The rental unit was full of extra youngsters. One might have been a cousin, maybe a goddaughter, or even later a grandchild, all spending the night, all made to feel welcome, all squeezed into this small yet upbeat family setting. A cousin, Deonce Jarvis, lived in the home for a decade after his father was sent away to prison. Everyone in the family turned very emotional the day Jarvis asked Gina and Tony Roy if he could call them mom and dad.

"To me, it was home and we loved it and it was comfortable," Jaamela Roy said. "We didn't feel it was too small. Even though we didn't grow up in a huge house, we weren't in the projects or the ghetto. We had a backyard to run around in. I guess there were so many of us that we were easily entertained."

Brandon Roy answered to unusual family obligations, too. This was especially true for a teenage boy with significant basketball prowess. On Fridays, his aunt Renee dropped off her clothes at the Delridge Way house and paid Brandon to iron them. He had everything neatly pressed and ready to return by Sunday night. He took this job seriously. When basketball commitments got in the way, Gina Roy stepped in and covered for him. She handed the clothes back without telling her sister-in-law how this task was completed. She always turned over the ironing money to her conscientious son. In return, Brandon made sure his mother was never short of cash.

"I always gave my mom money," he said. "If she needed fifteen dollars to buy some eggs and bread, I'd give it to her. I always worked to have money, but when I got it I didn't know what to do with it. I kept it in a shoebox."

With two athletic-minded sons, Tony and Gina Roy decided early on to get their kids involved on various teams, providing they could limit the time commitment required. Ed and Brandon were two years apart, but they played almost exclusively on the same youth teams. The reason: their parents didn't want to sit through two practices a day if they could avoid it. The Roys paired their boys together in every activity with the possible exception of football, which often separated the kids by weight. This meant Brandon usually played only with the older guys, and always had to find a way to fit in.

This also led to a unique sibling dynamic. Brandon made it a point to defer to his older brother at all times. Ed was the star of these teams, and there were no challenges or complaints issued by the submissive, if not loyal, little brother. Ed was loud and boisterous, Brandon introspective and sedate. Brandon readily accepted this role. In fact, he wouldn't play if Ed wasn't playing. He felt a sense of duty in this role.

"It wasn't that I had a problem taking a backseat; it's what I did," Brandon explained. "Ed was the best basketball player and I was the ninth guy on the team. When I was growing up, I never knew how good I was because I never played with guys my age. He was Batman and I was Robin, and I didn't mind being Robin."

"Edward was always the lead dog in the family," Tony Roy added. "Brandon was happy being the second dog and not noticed."

These brothers got involved in everything, initially signing up for indoor soccer and karate class, before turning to more traditional sports. At first, Tony Roy wouldn't let his sons play basketball, his favorite sport, in an organized manner, because he knew invariably what would happen. He understood how easy it was to become devoted to the hoop game at the expense of everything else, because that's what had happened to him. He wanted sporting variety in their young lives, and there was only one way to get it. "I kept them from basketball because I didn't want that being all they did," he said.

Brandon Roy's first athletic involvement was chasing a soccer ball around the gym at South Shore Middle School when he was four, followed by a karate class he shared with his brother, cousins, and an uncle. The siblings came home armed with trophies and awards from each activity. They always were willing to try something different; it's one reason they became such skilled athletes and loved to compete.

"Indoor soccer is still the [most fun] sport I ever played," Brandon Roy said. "I stopped playing when it moved outside, because it wasn't fun anymore then. It was, 'Can I play goalie today?' Sure. 'I want to play forward.' Sure. I liked the sport when it was just pure fun. It was innocent."

Roy would get involved in basketball soon enough and turn that passion into an NBA career. Yet the first sport in which he enjoyed any reasonable success, and drew attention to himself, was football. As a grade-schooler, he was a big running back with breakaway speed and all the moves. He was a natural at this game. This led some coaches later to ask: As a teenager or older, could this athletically gifted Brandon Roy have become a prolific runner? Could he have become a high school and college phenomenon? Could he have been another Adrian Peterson, only taller?

Roy aborted his first attempt at football. In the third grade, he turned out for the Rainier Eagles, won the job as a starting running back, and abruptly quit the team the night before the season-opening jamboree. Other kids were angry at Brandon because the game had come so easy for him and he had beaten them out and shifted the spotlight from them, and he sensed their animosity. Further tempering his disinterest, an uncle had died in an auto accident, someone with whom Brandon had shared his football experiences, and the game didn't seem nearly as fun without him.

Brandon still came to practice every day; he just played off to the side by himself, oblivious while Ed and his former Rainier teammates labored through the workouts and prepared for upcoming weekend games. His mother wasn't happy with her younger son's sudden decision to abandon football, and for good reason, but she didn't interfere.

"I borrowed money to get him a helmet and shoulder pads," Gina Roy pointed out.

For fourth and fifth grade, Brandon Roy decided to play football after all and he put on a backfield show for the Rainier Eagles. He drew all sorts of youth coaches and curious adults to his weekend football games. People treated these outings as must-see events at Rainier Playfield, a well-established proving ground for youngsters who later became NFL running backs, including Terry Metcalf, Charlie Mitchell, and Corey Dillon. Young Brandon Roy typically scored three or four touchdowns per game, often sprinting past everyone while turning in long runs. He built a playground reputation that circulated widely throughout Seattle's south end.

Will Conroy, a running back for the midtown Central Area Youth Association, better known as CAYA, first encountered Roy on the football field when he was eleven and Brandon was ten. Conroy wanted to meet this kid so skilled in running with a football and finding the end zone. From this early starting point, they became high school and college basketball teammates, good friends, and later even roommates. As with everyone, Brandon needed time to get comfortable with this confident new acquaintance.

"He was shy by nature," Conroy said. "After he warmed up to you, he could be the funniest guy in the room."

Roy always stood out in football, even at the annual awards banquet. In fourth grade, he reluctantly showed up dressed in a tuxedo. He took an active part in a family wedding before the football ceremony and his parents wouldn't let him change his clothes between events. Worse yet, he won a lot of awards that day, requiring him to continually parade up and down in front of his teammates in this overdressed manner, and hear about it, every step.

By playing football, Roy was able to express himself for the first time and step out of his brother's shadow. Typically laid-back, he surprised people with infrequent displays of emotion or even bravado, actions that generally ran counter to his otherwise stoic personality.

On one occasion, Roy scored a touchdown and drew snickers for mimicking the Heisman Trophy pose made famous by Desmond Howard, the University of Michigan wide receiver, punt returner, and 1991 Heisman recipient. It was the one-legged, one-arm-extended move that was copied by countless others, including the University of Washington's All-America wide receiver Mario Bailey, another Rainier Playfield alumnus, who pulled off his copycat moment a few years earlier in the Rose Bowl on national TV.

During another game, Roy broke free for several touchdowns, making sure his first trip to the end zone was the most memorable. Once he crossed the goal line, the fifth-grader dropped to one knee, said a prayer and crossed his chest in a gesture that was both symbolic and preplanned. The Rainier Eagles crowd responded enthusiastically, applauding and cheering him. Nearly everyone in attendance knew that Brandon's great-grandmother, Lucy Winzer, had died a few days before in her south Seattle senior assisted-living home. Her passing left family members upset and in mourning, particularly his grandmother, Frances, one of the people Brandon adored most. Without prodding, the concerned grandson decided on his own to show family support in some meaningful way during his football game.

"I wanted to do something when I scored the first touchdown, and I was nervous," Brandon Roy said. "I said a prayer for my great-grandma, but I said it more for my grandmother. I had never seen her sad before, and I wanted her to be back strong. It was the first time I had seen my grandmother down."

While football supplied him with plenty of confidence, Brandon gave up the sport after just two seasons when he entered the sixth grade. He enjoyed the games and touchdowns, but he didn't like practice or getting hit every day. He was a natural, but it wasn't enough to keep him in the helmet and shoulder pads his mother had scrambled to acquire. Besides, he played touch football during recess, getting his regular fill. He had other things he wanted to do with his time after school. He was just a kid. The action figures were still calling him. "I would rather play with my toys," he said unapologetically.

Brandon also tried swinging a bat. For fourth and fifth grade, he played Little League baseball for a Rainier Valley team named Burdick Locksmith, which was the sponsor. He was a shortstop, first baseman, and center fielder. In each game, he played alongside his brother. This made Frances Roy especially happy, because she loved the spring sport more than the others they played. Their grandmother was a huge Mariners fan. Not only that, she thought the Roy boys looked cute in their uniforms.

Yet with Brandon, there always seemed to be some pressing issue that wasn't easily resolved whenever he was on the baseball field. In one game, he needed to urinate in the worst way, even though he was next up. He raced to the restroom and back. With barely enough time to button up his pants and step up to the plate and even catch his breath, he smacked a grand-slam home run. As someone who tended to overanalyze things, he attributed this success to just swinging without thinking.

In another game, Brandon was upset and crying because his team was losing. His older brother walked over and told him to knock it off. The unrepentant Ed Roy was pitching that day and ready to take control of the game. He announced to his sniffling sibling that no one else was going to get a hit off him or even reach base that afternoon; he told him to wipe off those tears and play ball. Ed was good on his word. He struck out every batter he faced thereafter. He also hit a late, game-winning home run. There was no crying in baseball for the Roys, only eventual celebrating, as the older brother demonstrated in competitive fashion.

For another game, the assigned umpire didn't show and Tony Roy was pulled from the stands as a reluctant replacement. Of course, he experienced the worst thing that could happen for a stand-in arbiter with a family connection on the field. With Brandon at bat, Tony Roy called strike one. His son slugged the next pitch a long way, only to see it land foul. On the third pitch, Brandon let one zip past him in the strike zone with his bat sitting on his shoulder. His father hesitated before lifting his thumb, cringing all along.

"I looked over at Gina before I called it, but I had to call my boy out on strikes, and it killed me," Tony Roy recalled.

Baseball, too, fell by the wayside after the fifth grade. It had nothing to do with a questionable pitch call or Ed Roy's unsympathetic demands for immediate composure. Brandon and his brother finally were allowed to throw themselves into basketball, and they determined in a short period they had no time for anything else. Shooting hoops was all they wanted to do now, just as their dad had predicted. Basketball seemed more fun than the other sports.

That wasn't such a bad thing. Basketball rallied this family together more than ever. The Roy brothers would play for Rainier Valley, High Point, Delridge, and various Amateur Athletic Union teams, ultimately launching them toward Garfield High School. There would be revelations along the way. In grade school, a teacher pointed out that Brandon was ambidextrous after noticing that he easily wrote with both hands. He could play basketball with both, too. Unlike football and baseball, there was never any question about his commitment to this newfound sport. He could get both arms around it, and he was in it for the long run.

"I knew basketball was my love," Roy said. "I knew I would never walk away from basketball."

After playing first for a Rainier Valley team, the Roy brothers took their talents to the High Point Community Center on the opposite side of West Seattle from home. Willie Williams, who had coached their dad, expressed an interest in coaching the sons. They spent three years on teams headed up by Williams, a Chief Sealth High School football legend. Teaming with the older guys, Brandon seemed to fit in right away. Williams had seen him play and suggested that moving the younger brother up a couple of levels wasn't a far-fetched idea. The kid was coachable, a plus at any level of basketball. The head coach made the transition even easier by adding Tony Roy as the team's assistant coach.

Two years younger than most, Brandon was well liked by his teammates. They appreciated the fact that he shared the ball without having to be asked. They showed their gratitude by nearly voting him team captain one season. He finished second in the balloting, even receiving his older brother's vote, all of which was both a surprise and relief to his coaches, who had decided that one of the older players still needed to be the team leader.

Brandon Roy could wait for a much bigger role, to become the team centerpiece someday. It was clear that he and basketball were meant for each other. And it wouldn't be too long before this sporting choice would allow him to move out of the rental home at 4137 Delridge Way Southwest, and obtain that house with grass.

CHAPTER 4

BRANDON & NATE

Brandon Roy was the tall, quiet kid, someone who could easily blend into the background. Nate Robinson was the shorter one, who soon stopped growing, and displayed all brashness and hyperactivity from the beginning. They were eleven when they first met and became inseparable friends as fifth-graders at Rainier View Elementary School in south Seattle. They sat near each other in Soren Sorenson's class and used this opportunity to become well-acquainted. They were transfer students both new to the grade school for the 1994-95 school year. Early on, they probably enjoyed each other's company a little too much.

They talked all the time in class. They talked about playing basketball at recess. They talked about collecting basketball trading cards. At this tender age, they even talked about becoming NBA players together.

"With me and Brandon, we used to sit by each other and we used to talk every day," Robinson said. "We talked about what we wanted to be when we grew up, that we wanted to play basketball and we wanted to be famous. We always talked about that. It was just a daydream, just a whisper."

Still, they were heard loud and clear. They paid for their nonstop prattle, too. Forced to serve a noontime detention in one instance, their penalty was to write *I will not talk in class* one hundred times on the front blackboard in the class of their cranky teacher. Naturally this stern disciplinary measure turned into a spirited competition rather than all-out drudgery for these two. Robinson tried to write his sentences faster than Roy, who tried his best to keep pace.

"We used to race," Robinson said. "It was who could get it done the fastest. It helped us with our punishment and to get us through it."

"We competed at everything," Roy concurred. "Nate always was like that. I was a quiet competitor. He brought me into it, and I had to step it up."

Robinson was a fun-loving kid and the son of a former University of Washington football standout and Rose Bowl and Orange Bowl hero. Roy was more on the reserved side but a budding jokester just the same. Put them together, and mischief was certain to break out.

Even the simplest stuff got them revved up. Once, they were given an assignment to draw something and color it in. Of course, they went at this in class like two wild animals fighting over a piece of meat.

"We'd argue who was coloring better, who was drawing better," Roy said.

Rainier View Elementary School was perched on a ridge in south Seattle's Skyway neighborhood, a mile west and up the hill from Rainier Beach High School, Robinson's future destination. A well-worn place, the school could have used a little polish, if not some of the boys' coloring, on the exterior. It was a combination single- and two-story complex composed primarily of fading brick and surrounded on three of four sides by overgrown shrubbery. An aging wooden sign with the school name carved into it was fastened to the front wall of the building. A rusted flagpole stood erect in the circular drive that provided a student drop-off area.

In the back of the school were three portable classrooms and a spacious playground that seemed to run forever, which included a solitary basketball court. White backboards were mounted at each end. The court was nestled up against a chain-link fence and under the welcome shade of a towering tree. It was an extraordinary place to shoot hoops, if only for the simple matter that it was an early launching pad for these two strains of impending NBA royalty.

Roy and Robinson spent a lot of recess time in that right-hand corner of the schoolyard, tossing up shots and tossing out challenges to each other and others. In the mornings before class started, one of them always waited diligently at the basketball court for the other to arrive by bus.

Mr. Sorenson was an old-school teacher, someone who grew up on a central Washington farm and became a tough-love proponent in the big-city classroom. Formerly a civil-rights worker, he requested school work assignments that catered to predominantly black students at south Seattle schools, certain that he could do his most good as a teacher in this setting. He was dedicated to helping minority kids succeed, but hardly was a pushover, as those future pro basketball players could attest following their extensive noon-time chalkboard session. Test the limits with him, and you forfeited your lunch hour or recess.

"I used to say, 'I'll warn you one time and then you will do your business at your maximum inconvenience,' " Sorenson said.

Sorenson was soft on his students in one of his earliest teaching assignments at the Colman School, well before he arrived at Rainier View. The kids did their best to take advantage of him. The principal at that school said it was one of two cases in which he had seen a teacher lose complete control of a class. Sorenson took this to heart. In 1994-95, if he caught someone acting up in a hallway or on the playground, he would detain him or her against the nearest plaster or brick background and always yell out in animated fashion: "Hit the wall, tiger! I'll let you loose if you prove you're doing the right thing. If not, it's hit the wall, tiger!"

"We were scared of him, scared we'd get into trouble, and I already knew him," Roy said.

The teacher privately liked Robinson's wise-guy attitude, because that's what allowed Mr. Sorenson to make his way through school, first in rural Kittitas County and later Ellensburg in central Washington. Robinson was what the teacher described as "a hard head," someone stubborn and unafraid to take chances, which was how Sorenson approached his formative years. On the other hand, Roy seemed to meekly stand off to the side and rarely created a fuss for Sorenson, at times becoming almost indistinguishable among the rest of the student body.

Mr. Sorenson and Roy knew each other some. They both spent the previous three years at the nearby African American Academy, though never in the same classroom. Roy's mother worked in the school lunchroom, giving Brandon more profile than most kids who walked the hallways. Gina Roy moved him to Rainier View, deciding her second son and daughter Jaamela should have a public-school education, a decision based on economics. By chance, Sorenson ended up with them at the Roys' next scholastic stop.

"Brandon was much more quiet, as quiet and nice as the day is long," Sorenson said. "I remember the hard heads much more clearly. Nate liked the action, liked to stir stuff up. If there was no action, he had a tendency to create it. I was a hard head, too. I remember saying to myself about hard heads: 'These are my people.' If there was a ringleader at that point in their lives, it was Nate."

Little did these hoop-crazy fifth-graders realize that their sometimes-gruff teacher had a noteworthy college basketball connection in his family tree. Albertson Sorenson, Soren's great-uncle, played parts of five seasons and became a big star for Washington State University, most notably for the 1916-17 Cougars team that finished 25-1 and was proclaimed the national champion by the Helms Foundation poll. Sorenson had also taught an NBA-bound student before. Doug Christie, who later played for seven teams over fifteen pro seasons, was in one of his earlier elementary school classes in the south end.

If they managed to stay out of trouble, Roy and Robinson took their new-found friendship to the lunchroom and then outside to the playground. They sat together and ate lunch every day. They played basketball together without interruption, already forming a dream team while nowhere near their teenage years. There was no hesitation in taking on all comers, no matter how many there were on the other side or what sport might be involved, though basketball was a certain trigger for a pickup game.

"We used to play other kids two-on-five, and we used to beat them," Robinson said.

Both Roy and Robinson were newcomers to Rainier View that year, one reason they reached out to each other in such a dependent manner. They didn't know anyone else. They found comfort in their similar new-kid situations. While Roy was familiar with his fifth-grade teacher, he knew no one else who attended or worked at the grade school at 11650 Beacon Avenue South, initially making him reluctant to go there. The outgoing Robinson was a welcome sight.

"Nate was not only my best friend, he was like my only friend at that point," Roy recalled. "I wouldn't have had any other friends. We just clicked. If Nate and I didn't meet each other on the first day [of school], it was the second day."

The boys soon were holding sleepovers at each other's homes. Robinson lived in Rainier Valley, Roy a dozen miles away in West Seattle. They played pickup basketball games in Roy's driveway. Ironically, Robinson recruited his new friend to join him on a Delridge Community Center basketball team coached by that well-known father of his, Jacque. This was easy enough for Roy, because he lived just a half block from the community center gym. The difficult part for him was fitting in on the team. Roy felt shy around Nate's dad. He was so nervous he didn't play well or shoot much early on.

This reticence lasted for three games before Robinson, always the point-blank personality, urged his grade-school friend to climb out of his shell and show what he could do as a basketball player. Robinson had a great deal at stake here; his reputation for spotting hoop talent was on the line. He had told everyone what a good player Roy was, and now it was time for his school chum to produce in a big way to back up Robinson's boastful words.

"He said to me, 'Hey B, you've got to play, you've got to shoot,' " said Roy, who eventually became comfortable enough to become the league's best player. "He was not bashful at all."

As for the basketball cards, Roy and Robinson regularly traded with another classmate, a kid named Tony, whose vast collection included at least one card of every player in every sport. They couldn't compete with Tony, only engage in the occasional transaction with him, but they goaded each other over who had the better cards in their abbreviated sets. They were sneaky about this hobby, because it wasn't exactly penciled into the lean family budgets in each household.

Roy purchased individual cards out of a machine for a quarter and a pack of cards for ten quarters near his grandmother's Beacon Hill house. He kept the high-profile players and threw away the rest. He only wanted the stars, players such as Magic Johnson or Michael Jordan. The card collections allowed Roy and Robinson to dream a little more, and that led to ongoing debates about their sporting futures.

Robinson said he wanted it all, when and if he turned professional. He proclaimed that both basketball and football were likely future destinations for him, in large part because his father had played the latter and Nate preferred the former. This led to an entirely different sort of argument.

"I wanted to play for the Chicago Bulls because of Michael Jordan and that whole era," Roy pointed out. "Nate wanted to play in both the NFL and NBA. I said, 'I don't think you can do that.'"

They also shared a mutual love of football, though they never played together on the same team. That wasn't Nate's choice. Roy stopped playing for the Rainier Eagles after the fifth grade, just when Robinson was getting ready to join the same team. Robinson wanted them to become teammates again, but it wasn't going to happen.

"He loved the University of Miami, that was his football team, and he loved watching them," Robinson recounted vividly. "But then B-Roy started getting sort of tall and he stopped playing."

"He begged me to come back," Roy said. "I said, 'No, Nate, I did my football thing.' I was a basketball player who just happened to play football."

As these two future NBA players started hanging out at Rainier View, they weren't aware that their parents already knew each other from Seattle's Central Area. Nor was the older generation immediately plugged into the fact their sons had formed a close friendship and were running around together at the Skyway grade school.

Renee Busch, Robinson's mother, was pleasantly surprised the day she picked up Nate from school and her son pointed out Brandon Roy as his new buddy. She knew immediately who he was.

At Garfield High School, Renee Busch was Renee Hollingsworth, a dance-team member for the "Puffettes" and somebody who loved to entertain, just like her son. She was just a year older than Brandon's parents, Tony Roy and Gina Crawford. They were well acquainted.

"The parents already knew each other before they were born," Renee Busch said. "We were good friends, all of us. Back in the day, everybody hung real tight."

"As kids, we thought that was cool," Brandon Roy recounted. "We didn't know how small the world really was."

Robinson's high-level athleticism, specifically his often dazzling and entertaining footwork on the basketball floor, was considered an unquestioned gift handed down from the family gene pool built around appearances in two New Year's Day college bowl games. Few people, however, guessed correctly on the exact source of his nimbleness. The Roys had insider knowledge.

"Everybody thinks it was Jacque who gave him that," Gina Roy said. "It was his mom."

The closeness of the boys' friendship cooled once fifth grade was over. The younger Roy and Robinson were pulled apart for their middle school and high school years, ending up in different parts of the city. Even with open enrollment and the obvious lure of Garfield basketball, Renee Busch made her son stay close to home when it came to high school.

"I asked Nate, 'Your mom went to Garfield, why don't you?' " Roy said.

Busch knew exactly which high school was best suited for her and her son's needs. She wanted to keep transportation needs simple rather than have to cart him across the city to class every day. This was decided when Robinson got kicked off the McClure Middle School bus for unruliness. Before she could go to work, Busch had to drive him across town daily, through heavy traffic, and she vowed this wasn't going to happen again. Robinson was enrolled at Rainier Beach High School, so he could walk home every day if needed, permitting him room to get into trouble and not make his mother pay for it.

While Robinson was assigned to McClure, Roy enrolled at Hamilton Middle School in north Seattle because his brother Ed went there. Brandon also attended Meany Middle School for his second year before returning to Hamilton as an eighth-grader. Brandon and Nate still ran into each other, but it wasn't quite the same connection as before at Rainier View. There wasn't any opportunity for long conversations involving the NBA or any of those us-against-the-world basketball games at recess. There wasn't the daily competition between them, either.

"It was weird, because we both sort of left our best friends behind," Roy said. "I thought to myself and wished that Nate and I could get that relationship back. When we saw each other, I could tell he had new friends and he could tell I had new friends. We sort of went different ways."

They were pulled apart even more for high school. Robinson attended Rainier Beach as a freshman and senior, but spent his sophomore and junior years living with his father and attending James Logan High School in Union City, California. Taking advantage of Seattle's open enrollment policy, Brandon followed his brother to Garfield. After suiting up for so many different Rainier Valley teams in every sport, Roy assumed he was going to attend and play basketball for Franklin High. He had competed steadily against Central Area Youth Association teams that typically funneled players to Garfield, teams he had grown to despise every year in competitive fashion. He was in for a huge surprise, however, once his brother was ready to leave middle school and his parents weighed the next step.

Roy understood that his parents had attended Garfield High. His brother was either going to enroll there or attend a Catholic school. Roy needed a moment to comprehend this academic plan. It ran counter to everything he had envisioned.

"I thought I was a Quaker," Brandon said. "The rivalry is Rainier and Central, and people think the rivalry starts in high school, but it's as kids. Growing up, I realized I was on the wrong side of the rivalry. When they said if Ed didn't go to O'Dea, he was going to Garfield, I said, 'Where did that come from?' I realized I was all turned around."

Size likewise sent Roy and Robinson in opposing directions as soon as they entered their teenage years. Topping out at a quarter inch under six-foot-six by high school, Roy ultimately grew nearly a foot taller than his friend.

"I was kind of normal then," Nate said. "But Brandon kept going and I just stopped."

Roy and Robinson grew up and moved away from Rainier View Elementary and their cherished playground court, but they never really let go of that enchanting fifth-grade year. Talking too much, writing about it in chalk and in a hurry, and daydreaming about a pro basketball future was an education in itself.

Chapter 5

The Garfield Years

Want to play basketball for Garfield High School? Get in line. When Brandon Roy was in school, it stretched perhaps one hundred and thirty players deep. This nonstop procession of tryout candidates could have backed out the purple gymnasium door and down the steps, through the parking lot, across Twenty-third Avenue and wrapped itself around Ezell's Famous Chicken restaurant a couple of times. The first cut was to one hundred, on the way to forty-five or fifty players generously filling out the rosters of the Bulldogs' varsity, junior varsity, and sophomore basketball teams.

"Everybody wanted to be a Bulldog," Garfield point-guard Marques Echols said. "It was tradition."

Advised to pare the kids to a workable number right away, Garfield coach Wayne Floyd always delayed the inevitable and let everybody hang around for a week, just to give them a taste of the most successful and revered schoolboy program in Washington state. Everyone at the school who possessed anything that remotely resembled a credible jump shot wanted a chance to show what he could do and be part of this elaborate weeding-out process.

"It was incredible, man," Floyd recounted. "A lot of guys knew they weren't going to make it, but they wanted to be on the floor with players like Will Conroy and Roydell Smiley and guard them and get dunked on by them, just to say they were dunked on."

Brandon and Floyd were introduced two years earlier at Nate McMillan's Back to School Camp held at Chief Sealth High School, a somewhat ironic meeting place considering McMillan later would become Roy's NBA coach in Portland. Floyd was the camp's lead director when this eighth-grader and his parents approached him. Brandon wanted the coach to know he was coming to Garfield soon to play for him. Tony Roy wanted Floyd to know he was getting his youngest son and another talented player.

Garfield had earned eleven boys' state championships, which was more than any other school at any other level, and almost double the next 4A team, Walla Walla High School. This run of unparalleled hardwood success started with the first title won by a Doug Smart-led team in 1954-55, landing Smart a University of Washington scholarship. It was highlighted by arguably the state's most dominant prep basketball team ever assembled, Garfield's frighteningly powerful and unbeaten "Super Dogs" in 1973-74. Garfield basketball exploded under the capable coaching hands of former Seattle SuperSonics guard Al Hairston, who had coached Brandon's father and whose teams collected five championships in a dozen years.

The games were a source of pride for one of Seattle's oldest high schools, located in the heart of the city. The gym was always overheated with plenty of attitude and energy, particularly if a south-end rival such as Franklin High School or Rainier Beach High School paid a visit.

As a sophomore, Brandon Roy didn't have any trouble making the Bulldogs' 1999-2000 varsity roster and becoming part of this wintertime main attraction. It helped having an older brother who was an all-state selection for a state championship club and was ready to become a three-year starter. It helped having a father who was an all-Metro honorable-mention selection for Garfield eighteen years earlier. It helped having sufficient basketball talent surrounding him, especially on this team. The Bulldogs squad had so much firepower, six of the eleven players on the 2000 state tournament roster would receive Division I college scholarships, and two of them would play in the NBA.

For his first varsity game against Sammamish High School, Roy settled into a seat on the bench, happy enough to be wearing Garfield's fancy purple and white warm-ups and classic uniform. He was content to be part of this elite team, to have a front-row vantage point from which to watch his older brother in action. He wasn't expecting to play much, if at all, in the season opener. Of course, only a few minutes had been played when he was summoned by Floyd, and he came off the bench as a substitute player.

Garfield fans had a natural inclination to compare the Roy brothers and their games. Entering his final season, Ed Roy had been a sophomore starter and all-tournament selection for the 1997-98 Bulldogs team that won the school's most recent state championship over Tacoma's Wilson High. He was a program mainstay. Ed had been taller and stronger as a sophomore than Brandon was as a tenth-grader. Ed's game depended on power and intimidation. Brandon's basketball approach was more about finesse and fitting in. Brandon was relegated to a reserve role in his first varsity season while also required to pull a few weekly minutes for the JV team, ensuring that he didn't sit idle; he drew enough time between the two squads to progress as a player. Brandon was a decent player, he just wasn't as advanced as his brother at the same age.

"I could tell he was a good player, but I didn't look at him and say, 'Damn, he was going to be good,' " Floyd said. "If anybody thought they saw him as an NBA player at that time, I wouldn't have believed them."

The 1999-2000 Bulldogs were so cocky and confident they promoted themselves as a mini-version of the University of Cincinnati Bearcats, the college game's flashiest team and a serious NCAA championship contender that season. All of the Bulldogs players wore black basketball shoes, black socks, and as much black as possible, same as Cincy. Each of the starters adopted one of the Bearcats headliners and tried to portray him on the court. Ed Roy chose Kenyon Martin, Simmons was DerMarr Johnson, Conroy identified with Kenny Satterfield, and so it went through the first five.

"They were the best team in the nation and we were the best team in the state," Conroy said.

Garfield won its first twenty-one games before losing to Franklin High School that year; Cincinnati captured twenty-four of its first twenty-five games. The Bulldogs' Michael Thompson, a starting guard, broke a finger that ended his season the same night that the Bearcats' Martin fractured his right leg, canceling out the rest of his season, too. Both teams were eliminated from a postseason tournament within twenty-four hours of each other. Cincy lost in the Conference USA Tournament in a shocking upset, 68-58, to a Saint Louis University team coached by Lorenzo Romar, soon to become Brandon Roy's college coach; the Bulldogs were ousted from the 4A state boys' basketball tournament the next night, falling 54-52 to Tacoma's Foss High School. The similarities were uncanny.

When they weren't attempting to impersonate the Bearcats, Garfield players playfully answered to another label that emerged from the phonetic they shared: Ed Roy, Brandon Roy, Will Conroy, Roydell Smiley.

"We used to call ourselves the Roy brothers," Brandon Roy said.

The younger Roy had to pay some serious dues just to get through that sophomore year. As a kid known for his unwavering good citizenship, he drew a rare smudge on his record when he was involved in a brief scuffle in the gym with another student, over something innocuous with someone whose name he no longer recalls. Ed Roy had just walked out of the gym when the other combatant offered an insult to his younger brother that included a mother reference. Brandon socked him in the nose, knocking him to the ground. Ed Roy walked back inside to find the mouthy guy lying on the floor.

"We weren't bad kids, but we made sure we weren't going to get picked on," Ed Roy said.

Brandon and his adversary were escorted to the office by a school security guard. It was the worst trouble Roy had encountered. He was handed a three-day suspension from school. His punishment doled out by Floyd was painful, too—a weeklong suspension from the Garfield varsity team. He was forced to sit out four Christmas tournament games, and pull a mandatory half-game of service for the Bulldogs' JV team in a game at Juanita High School.

Floyd also scolded Roy for his actions, informing him rather pointedly that the school's varsity basketball players had an image to maintain and they just didn't get into fights on campus. The player feared added repercussions after this conversation.

"I thought, 'Oh, man, he's going to put me back on the junior varsity for the season,' " he said.

His trouble behind him, Roy averaged 5.7 points per game and drew significant minutes among Garfield's star-studded cast. Smiley, a senior swingman who would later play for the University of Southern California, was the team's leading scorer with 16.2 points per game, Ed Roy was next with 14.6, and Simmons, another eventual University of Washington player, checked in with 12.4.

The younger Roy brother was a support piece, but he had privileges because of his family ties. Center Anthony Washington wanted to wear No. 4 that season, but Ed Roy, who wore No. 3, thought the number better suited his little brother, who wasn't at practice that day. Typically, single-digit numbers were the most desired on the high-school level for good reason: the higher the number worn by players often corresponded with fewer minutes played. Washington, who would later play for the University of Washington and Portland State University, chose it because NBA player Chris Webber, his favorite player, wore No. 4. The Garfield big man reluctantly yielded and settled for No. 12, which Washington considered a point-guard number. Ed Roy did all of the negotiating. Brandon wore No. 4 for two of his three Garfield seasons, changing to No. 23 for a season because it was Michael Jordan's number.

"I was a little upset, but I understood," Washington said of one Roy sibling providing interference for the other. "Ed always was kind of looking out for his brother, and that's what he was supposed to do. Ed won state his sophomore year and was already a legend. If his little brother wanted to wear that number, he was going to wear that number. Ed was the leader. He was like [Charles] Barkley. He could be a monster in his day. I respected their wishes."

The Roys were usually on a tight budget, but the brothers' needs were simple: Air Jordan basketball shoes. Some pairs were collectors' items put on display at home; other pairs were used in games. Ed Roy wore size eighteen, jumping two shoe sizes in two months as his body started to sprout in a hurry when he was a fifteen-year-old. Brandon pulled on size fifteens. The siblings lined up their coveted footwear on closet shelves rather than wear it, much to the dismay of their hardworking father. He wanted to pull them on and give all the shoes a test run.

"The one thing I let them indulge in, the *only* thing I let them indulge in, were Jordans," Gina Roy said. "I wanted them to stay kids as long as possible."

Garfield's top-ranked team took a 22-1 record into the 2000 state tournament and won its first two games. This included a 51-42 second-round victory over Mountlake Terrace High School, a game in which Brandon Roy served up one of his first attention-getting moments for the Bulldogs—he drove the baseline and explosively tossed down a two-handed dunk on forward Seamus Boxley, later a Division I player for Portland State University.

A marquee semifinal matchup against Foss High School at the Tacoma Dome came next. This game led young Brandon Roy to one of the most challenging moments of his basketball career at any level. With 1.9 seconds left to play against the Falcons, he was fouled and sent to the line with two shots to tie a highly competitive game and push it into overtime. He bounced the ball a few times, took aim, and let fly with the first attempt. It caromed off the front rim. Roy grabbed his head in horror with both hands. A time-out was called. As his coach tried to outline a play to rescue the game, the younger brother was in basketball shock.

Roy was told to purposely miss the next shot to the right while his brother and Smiley crossed inside to confuse the defenders. The shaken sophomore did this on command. Both seniors put a hand on the ball, but their tips didn't drop. The final horn sounded. The Bulldogs were done. Foss went on to win the title and Garfield finished third in state.

As he left the floor, Brandon Roy briefly made eye contact with his mother, who was standing in the crowd with a sympathetic look on her face. In the hallway outside the Bulldogs' locker room, he saw Ed Roy, with his jersey pulled up over his head to hide disappointment, and fell apart. Convinced he let his brother down and cost him another state championship, the sophomore dropped to the floor in despair, lying face-down for a few moments. His brother, however, made sure Brandon wasn't left alone to suffer long.

"He picked me up off the ground and said, 'It wasn't your fault,'" Brandon recounted. "I said, 'Yes, it was. I missed a free throw.' He said, 'Dude, I missed a point-blank tip.' All that time I thought he was mad at me, and he was mad at himself. We sat there for thirty minutes. We didn't come out until halftime of the next game."

"I never wanted my brother to feel that bad," Ed Roy said. "I would deal with it. I didn't want that taste in his mouth. I had tasted it before. I put one arm around him and said, 'Little brother, I'm going to take care of you.' We never should have been in that situation. I should have taken over the game."

The missed free throw had such a deep impact on Roy, he wrote multiple school papers about it in the months that followed. He described the sights, sounds, and feeling of the dread involved. He talked about the missed shot every chance he got. He would never forget it. It shook him to his soul. He envisioned himself as a money player, and he had gone broke on this play against Foss.

It wouldn't take Roy long to find himself in a similar pressure situation in a less intimidating atmosphere. Against an Amateur Athletic Union (AAU) team from California that summer in a near-empty gym, he went to the line to shoot three free throws inside the final nine seconds, with his summer team down by six points. He wondered to himself whether he had it in him to respond in a positive manner this time. Roy not only dropped in each critical shot, he had enough moxie to hit a three-pointer at the buzzer after a turnover to force overtime. His basketball confidence had returned in a huge way.

**

To get his game on track, Roy often turned to the AAU, particularly coach Lou Hobson, to find answers. He was an unpolished teenager getting ready to enroll at Garfield High when he met Hobson for the first time. Roy had been hurt, humbled, and unable to get over the hump as a basketball player leading up to this union. In 1998, he had developed tendinitis in both knees, a painful condition that limited his mobility and had to be addressed. He sat out his Hamilton Middle School basketball season to allow the chronic joint inflammation to dissipate and waited until he could join his Rotary Boys & Girls Club AAU team in the spring.

Rejoining Rotary, Roy was virtually ignored while trying to get back into basketball shape. He was treated as damaged goods in that spring of 1998. He was used sparingly, unexpectedly designated as the tenth or eleventh man on the AAU team. This was hard on everyone's ego in the family. He came off the bench only at the end of a woeful blowout. He was frustrated and his dad was angry. By halftime of the next game, Brandon hadn't played at all. An impatient Tony Roy suggested they leave the gym and go home. They headed for the exit, only to be intercepted by Hobson, coach of Team Yes, another local AAU entry. Let me work with him, Hobson proposed. The Roys were agreeable to this.

In terms of hoop status, Brandon sacrificed a lot by changing AAU teams. Rotary players wore fancy uniforms and had all of the latest basketball accessories. Team Yes wore T-shirts and mismatched uniforms and had access to only the bare necessities. Rotary supposedly catered to the city's best players, among them future Division I college prospects such as twins Lodrick and Rodrick Stewart (USC and USC, University of Kansas), Erik Bond (University of California, Saint Mary's College), Jeffrey Day (Washington, Creighton University), Errol Knight (Washington, Gonzaga University), and Nate Robinson (Washington). Team Yes offered a roster of hardworking players who didn't command a lot of college recruiting attention.

The deal-maker for Roy was the demanding Hobson, formerly an O'Dea High School head coach and Franklin High assistant coach. Hobson had worked individually with many of the Central Area's top basketball players, most notably Jason Terry, a Franklin alumnus who won a national championship at the University of Arizona and had gone on to play in the NBA for the Atlanta Hawks and Dallas Mavericks. Hobson now had Brandon Roy in his stable.

"That was the first time I had a coach who really got after me, and he used to get after me a lot," said Roy, who, after regaining his basketball legs, rejected an invitation from a conciliatory Rotary to return as well as an offer to join the high-profile Gary Payton All-Stars. "I felt a sense of loyalty to Lou. He got the most out of me as a player. He demanded the most out of me as a player."

Hobson was an acquired coaching taste, if not a shock to the system for some players. Point blank in his dealings, the coach told his kids to pull up their pants, keep their hair neat, and refrain from using any street-gang banter in his presence. If they wanted to be successful, he could help them. If they couldn't abide by his demands, they should go elsewhere and play. He made Roy a special project, enamored with the possibilities that this lean, graceful player presented.

"I did get after him because of all the kids I worked with, I thought early on he had the best chance to go beyond college basketball," Hobson said.

Roy turned in a breakout first season with Team Yes. He could pull the trigger on any dunk. He played some of his best games that summer on the national circuit. He landed on numerous AAU all-tournament teams. He came home and lined up a slew of trophies in his bedroom. Yet he still wasn't getting much publicity or outward respect around Seattle, not if the latest recruiting rankings, which leaned heavily to the Rotary players, were to be believed. Roy was an incoming freshman at Garfield, supposedly the trendy place to play high-school basketball, and now Rainier Beach High School, after a run of success behind clever guard Jamal Crawford and the emergence of the Stewart twins, was staking a claim to that reputation.

"I told Brandon to forget the hype, that the twins were rated and he wasn't, and to just stay the course," Hobson said.

When Seattle's elite AAU teams openly pursued Roy's services, a concerned Hobson called the family to see if he was going to lose his top player. Tony Roy assured the coach that Brandon was staying put. Hobson reminded them he still was offering only a T-shirt for a uniform top. Tony Roy passed this information along to his son. Make mine an extra large, Brandon responded.

Brandon Roy matured rapidly on the basketball floor. He made a good AAU team look great in national tournaments against the likes of the New York Gauchos, New York Riverside, and various North Carolina entries, all powerhouse teams headlining the summer circuit. Roy showed up Shavlik Randolph, a Duke University-bound player who was considered the nation's No. 1 high school player among the class of 2002. He went through his own growth spurt, shooting up five inches between his ninth- and tenth-grade years. He built a national following he didn't know about.

"He was in the same high school senior class as me, 2002," said Carmelo Anthony, who played for a Virginia prep school before turning to Syracuse University for one season and an NCAA championship and then jumping to the NBA's Denver Nuggets. "I saw him play a couple times in AAU. I always thought he had a nice game."

Word finally began to circulate around Seattle that there was a kid out there with exceptional basketball skills who was getting better and taller all the time, and it wasn't necessarily one of the much-advertised Stewart twins. People wanted to know more. A three-on-three game involving some curious basketball luminaries was arranged for Roy in the Wyckoff Gymnasium located on the grounds of Saint Joseph Church.

This was a popular inner-city basketball haven supervised by Hobson in Seattle's Capitol Hill neighborhood. Everybody referred to the recently built basketball gym, hidden behind a stately and sprawling church with an illuminated steeple, simply as "Saint Joe's." On this day, the fifteen-year-old kid from Garfield High was mixed in with Jamal Crawford and Terry, now both established NBA players from Seattle. An hour later, the pros walked away from the pickup game convinced Roy was something special.

"Brandon Roy was the one who stood out," Terry recalled. "He was the one with the NBA moves. He was the one with the ability."

***

Thanks to his AAU connections, Roy entered his junior season at Garfield High with his confidence restored and ready to take on a more prominent role; plus he had grown three inches. Even with four starters graduated from the previous team, the 2000-01 Bulldogs were ranked No. 1 once again in the preseason state polls. They carried that sort of mystique. Everybody assumed they would be good year after year. Roy was hailed as the school's next great player and topped this team in scoring with an 18.7 points-per-game average, fellow junior Marcelus Kemp was next with 17.7, and Conroy followed with 14.5 per game. With Ed Roy gone, Brandon was the designated team centerpiece, and he accepted this role, no longer reliant on his brother.

"Brandon was a pretty smart guy," Bulldogs assistant coach Dave Belmonte said. "At Garfield, sometimes you have to wait your turn. Brandon was comfortable. He could see his time coming."

Roy's lunchtime dunking exhibitions were almost more entertaining than Garfield's games. With his added height and advanced athleticism, there wasn't a shot he couldn't stuff through the rim. There might have been one hundred people in the gym each day, playing pickup basketball at the noon hour, unwilling to return to class until they were treated to one of Roy's creations at the end of the forty-five-minute break. People asked for his dunk of the week and he would make something up on the spot. Following NBA All-Star weekend, Roy showed up at school on Monday and provided an exact replica of Vince Carter's 360-degree windmill effort that had won the nationally televised dunk contest.

"He had crazy hops, ridiculous hops," Washington said. "Everybody was talking about Vince Carter, and he laced up his shoes and proceeded to do Vince Carter dunks like it was nothing."

Each day, Garfield gym manager Joe Bland had to raise the six baskets in the gym to shoo everyone out after the noon break. Roy used this moment as a creative prop. The last basket was pulled up to eleven feet, leaving it seemingly unplayable. Roy ran in and dunked easily. After Bland cranked to twelve feet, thinking this would get everyone back to class, Roy dunked again. With the basket height and degree of difficulty involved, his peers couldn't believe what they had just witnessed.

"There was a time I thought I was one of the highest jumping dudes in the world," Roy said.

"We were all amazed," Garfield teammate Alex Hatzey said. "That's when we knew he was at another level."

Roy's dunks brought him several temporary nicknames, such as Jackrabbit and Switch (for his ability to turn this talent on and off). He named these shots himself. Roy referred to one combination of moves as "Fruit Punch."

"Brandon was a boy in a man's body now," said Cole Allen, a Bulldogs teammate and close buddy.

The 2000-01 Garfield team was 24-1 entering the state tournament, a record that included four victories over Franklin and future NBA guard Aaron Brooks; one of those was a 100-51 pasting of the city rival at midseason. The regular season was marred only by an 84-83 overtime loss to Rainier Beach and the highly publicized Stewart twins on a late goaltending call.

The Bulldogs' top-ranked team drew Foss again in the tourney's first round, setting up an electrifying rematch. Yet the Falcons spoiled another steamroller season for Garfield, sneaking off with an 85-82 overtime victory at the Tacoma Dome. Sports writers and officials were in general agreement that it was the best played high school game in state history.

Roy scored a team-high twenty-five points in the postseason classic, but his coach wasn't completely happy with his top player's performance that day. The junior spent too much time out on the perimeter, whereas Floyd wanted him at the high post, his back to the basket, ready to create. They argued much of the game. This might have been the only time the unselfish Roy drew a coach's complaint about his playing approach.

"Brandon and I didn't see things eye-to-eye that game," said the Garfield coach, whose Bulldogs finished fifth in the 2000-01 state tournament. "People were telling him to face the basket, and asking him, 'Why does Floyd have you at the foul line?' In essence, he played out of position most of the game. We had intense discussions, at halftime and after the game."

Said Roy, "If I could go back and now see what he was seeing, I would agree."

Jaamela Roy, Roy's sister, offered an even more revealing view of a player experiencing a lot of success in a hurry and learning how to handle it. "In high school, as a junior and senior, Brandon got a little cocky," she said. "In college, he was back to himself."

By now, Roy had moved up to the top of all of the Division I recruiting lists. Unfortunately, he was falling behind in the classroom. His grades weren't very good. Something needed to be done for Roy, especially to keep his college basketball options intact. There was no easy solution. He wasn't trying to sabotage his academics. He wasn't skipping out on school. He wasn't purposely negligent. He had trouble keeping pace, and there was a legitimate reason.

"Brandon had a learning disability," Floyd said. "I never had a problem with him not going to class and not doing his homework. School was hard for him. He did the best he could."

"It took him a lot longer to process," said Jenni Maughan-MacDonald, former Garfield teacher and later a West Seattle High School assistant principal. "If it took someone five minutes to get something, it took him twice as long. He would get frustrated from time to time, because he didn't know why it was happening."

"I needed more time to read a book," Roy acknowledged.

The Garfield girls' basketball team had the gym reserved for practice immediately after school, leaving the boys with spare time on their hands before engaging in their daily workouts. Floyd strongly encouraged Isaiah Stanback, Echols, Kemp, Conroy, and Roy, all college-bound athletes in line for scholarships, to attend an extra, after-hours study hall four times a week for an academic boost. Beginning at 2:30 p.m., everyone met in Room 221.

They were tutored by Maughan-MacDonald, a young, vibrant teacher who was fascinated by their personalities and thought processes. They went over math and science homework together. They talked about school and life. They talked about the higher standards of conduct that athletes were held to. The boys talked about girls, and she listened and rolled her eyes.

"We learned a lot from each other," Maughan-MacDonald said. "I got to learn more about their lives and their struggles and what their needs were, and we were pretty open and honest about things. It was me, this little white girl from the north end, with them. How would any of us know these kids would go on and do what they did?"

Stanback, who became a starting quarterback for the University of Washington and an NFL wide receiver and kick returner for the Dallas Cowboys and New England Patriots, was the prim and proper one, unwilling to test any limits imposed. Conroy, who played in the NBA for four teams, wanted to push as many buttons as possible. He'd show up late and ask his tutor what she was going to do about it. Roy, the third future pro athlete in this bunch, fell somewhere in between those two, cautious yet overly inquisitive.

"He was always very nice and very thoughtful, but sometimes he would question things," Maughan-MacDonald said of Roy. "We wouldn't get into arguments, but he would push boundaries a little, like why is it like this or why is it like that?"

If he didn't always get his Garfield homework done properly, Brandon at least helped others complete theirs. His younger cousin, Brandi Roy, asked him to be the subject of her class project at Denny Middle School. This assignment required him to make a personal appearance at an after-school fair. He sat in her booth from 4-8 p.m., showing off his basketball shoes and patiently answering everyone's questions. Other kids chose science projects and offered homemade displays; Brandi selected her cousin and brought the real thing for people to examine. She also was asked to write a school paper describing the most influential person in her life. She decided that was Brandon.

Roy's basketball career, which had gone so well for three years since his bout with tendinitis, received a temporary setback in the summer of 2001. During a University of Washington team basketball camp set up to cater to full high school teams rather than individuals, Roy injured his left knee. He had a partial meniscus cartilage tear and tried to play through it. He sat out the ensuing Nike Camp because it was too rigorous. He would play sporadically for his AAU team thereafter, active for one game and sidelined for the next.

Roy waited two weeks for the swelling to go down and then accompanied his AAU team to the Big Time Tournament in Las Vegas with a definitive plan. He was determined to show college recruiters he was healthy. He dunked on several opponents once he saw several big-name coaches come through the door. He purposely drew a lot of attention to himself. At a subsequent Los Angeles-area tournament, Roy supplied added proof that his knee wasn't an issue. He was surrounded in the post by two taller players from a Flint, Michigan, team, when he tossed the ball off the backboard simply to keep from traveling, and in one remarkable, athletic motion caught it and dunked on both guys.

To be safe, Roy submitted to arthroscopic knee surgery before the summer was out. He had no court limitations afterward. Yet he was never quite the imaginative and unrestrained dunker again. Some of it was athleticism forever lost by the surgical intrusion. Some of it was by design.

"There was a stretch I was only known as a jumper, so I shied away from it," Roy said. "I wanted to be known as a good player."

A heavily recruited player, Roy chose to stay home and play college basketball, accepting a scholarship offer from the University of Washington and coach Bob Bender. Roy's decision ran counter to that of previous high-profile local players who had fled Seattle for programs with better national reputations. Yet he liked Bender, was enamored with a roster filled mostly with Seattle players, and wanted to stay home. Roy turned to his senior season at Garfield and another run at a state championship. Roy and Kemp were the only returning starters. The Bulldogs again were ranked No. 1 in the preseason state polls. Stanback, the future NFL player, was a new starter. Terrence Williams, a future NBA player, just a freshman, and Roy's old Delridge Way neighbor, was a new teammate and a reserve.

Garfield was primarily a two-man team offensively. Roy averaged 24.9 points, Kemp 19.5. No one else scored more than six points per game. Without a strong supporting cast, Roy learned to turn his game on whenever necessary. He broke open a tight contest against Roosevelt High School by throwing down a reverse dunk on two opposing players, followed by another ferocious dunk. Against Bothell High School, the Bulldogs were trailing by fifteen in the second half when Roy scored twenty points over a quarter and a half to pull out another victory. Teammates could count on him to bail them out on an individual basis, too.

"If we got caught in the air, we'd literally just throw the ball toward the hoop and Brandon would be there for a dunk," Alex Hatzey said. "I'd get caught in the air, throw the ball up in the air and it was, 'Superman's coming.' "

Roy wasn't afraid to assume the role of team enforcer, same as his brother had done when they played together. Meeting Portland's Jefferson High School in the annual Martin Luther King Tournament in Seattle, he watched as the visitors ran to the Bulldogs' midcourt logo in a group and stomped and pounded on it at the end of pregame introductions. The Garfield gym was packed. There were TV cameras poised to follow the action between two highly regarded Northwest teams. The atmosphere was electric. Yet this was a blatant form of intimidation, if not poor sportsmanship. Disturbed by the logo disrespect, Roy grabbed one of the visitors from behind by the legs and dragged him from the pile, leaving other players from each team to push and shove each other briefly before everyone was separated and play commenced.

With the game underway, Garfield's Echols led a two-on-one fast break down the floor. He caught sight of Roy coming up in a hurry from behind. The point guard reached the foul line and tossed a lob pass in the air, left to guess when and if Roy would catch up. Jefferson's Brandon Lincoln, who later played for the University of Oregon, got his hands on the ball first. Roy, however, ripped it from his grasp, dunked with emphasis, and the home crowd went wild.

The Garfield coach had no qualms with any of his seniors' actions, especially since they helped inspire the Bulldogs to a tough 76-71 victory.

"It showed him sticking up for the school," Floyd said. "It was nothing bad. He was usually a quiet leader. They were disrespecting us and he stepped up."

In the crowd was Martell Webster, a Seattle Preparatory School freshman, three years younger and watching Roy let it all hang out for the first time. This was one future pro watching another, though Webster didn't know it at the time.

"I don't think anybody really knew he was going to be that good," said Webster, who reached the NBA first and later welcomed Roy as a Portland Trail Blazers teammate. "He just kept working on his game and really improved. He kind of blew everybody away."

Roy also could be funny. Early in the season, the Bulldogs were entered in the Iolani Classic, a holiday tournament in Hawaii, matched up against a well-known Maryland team, Montrose Christian School. Roy and Stanback watched the other side run through warm-ups, trying to decide defensive matchups. All of a sudden, six-foot-eight Linas Kleiza, an NBA-bound forward after playing for the University of Missouri, grabbed a ball, let out a scream, and raced in for a ferocious, two-handed slam, meant to intimidate the Seattle players. "That's your man," Roy told Stanback. On the same trip, Roy walked through a park with Stanback and Kemp and had teammates running for safety after telling them of the killer mongoose he had read about that were sure to be roaming the area.

"He's real chill, but when he gets around the guys he's a real clown," Stanback said.

Entering the state tournament as a senior, Roy was the leading scorer in the sixteen-team field, topping an impressive collection of individuals who could hoist and hit. All of them had college basketball scholarships or baseball contracts. Included were Gonzaga-bound Adam Morrison (24.3 points per game) of Mead High School and Sean Mallon (24.2) of Ferris High School, Richland High School's Travis Buck (20.2), and the University of Oregon-bound Aaron Brooks (16.9) from Franklin High School. Morrison and Brooks, of course, were on the fast track to the NBA. Buck became an outfielder for the Oakland A's, Cleveland Indians, and Houston Astros. This tournament usually showcased a lot of top-notch athletes whose talents extended well beyond basketball. Ed Roy previously played state games against Cascade High's Grady Sizemore, who went on to become a Cleveland outfielder, and Wilson High's Marcus Trufant, later a Seattle Seahawks cornerback.

For all their good intentions in 2001-02, the Bulldogs, after compiling a 20-3 regular-season record, didn't survive this state tourney any better than the previous two. They easily captured their opener over Spokane's Shadle Park High School, but in the process lost Kemp to a broken foot, which proved disastrous. They didn't have Terrence Williams, either, because much to his consternation, faulty grades had made the ninth-grader ineligible once the regular season ended.

"If he had been eligible, we could have put him in the game with Brandon when Marcelus went down and I think we would have been okay," Floyd said.

For the third consecutive tourney, Garfield was eliminated by a Tacoma team in Tacoma. The Bulldogs came up short with their shorthanded lineup to the Lincoln High School Abes, 67-48, falling to the defending and soon-to-be repeating state champion. All the other side had to do was blanket Roy defensively to advance.

Two days later, the Garfield standout closed out his high-school career by ringing up a career-best thirty-eight points in a 71-70 victory over Snohomish High School and future college teammate Jon Brockman, good for a fourth-place state finish. Roy got a bigger thrill watching Allen's last-second block of a Brockman shot, preserving the outcome in their final outing together. Capturing an elusive state title was the only thing that could have made it better.

"I thought we could have won five in a row, three in a row for sure," Floyd said.

"We tried to dominate every game," Roy said.

Roy's collective Garfield record, even without bringing home the big hardware, was an impressive 75-8. Most wins were blowouts. Three of the losses were in overtime. Two were in the state semifinals. Something always went wrong at the worst possible time for the Bulldogs. But it was character-building stuff.

Roy had come back from a knee injury and overcome the Foss free-throw debacle, but he still hadn't convinced everyone that he carried a skill set that paralleled the best players in his senior class. He wasn't invited by the organizers of the McDonald's All-American Game. It was that kind of snub that kept him motivated to become a better basketball player.

"A lot of guys are more athletic and a lot of guys are more this and that, getting more publicity and getting all the accolades," said Alvin Snow, who played at Franklin High and Eastern Washington University. "He tells you he prides himself in being the underdog."

Roy now possessed a series of unique canine pedigrees: Underdog, Bulldogs, and his next stop, the Washington Huskies.

Chapter 6

Hair Jordan

Their first meeting was awkward. Make that embarrassing. Horrifying even. Brandon Roy was a junior, Tiana Bardwell a freshman, when stumbling efforts were made to bring them together at a Garfield High football game at Memorial Stadium in downtown Seattle. They sat in separate groups in the stands. The crossover began when Roy's brother Ed, a recent Garfield graduate who had returned from a brief stay at college, went over to speak with one of Bardwell's friends. Not so smoothly, Ed took note of Bardwell and told her that she was cute and she should meet his younger sibling. He had heard his brother mention her name before. Making matters worse, Ed impetuously asked for her phone number to pass along. It was difficult to determine who was more uncomfortable with this impromptu *Friday Night Lights* matchmaking: Brandon or Tiana?

"I went to my mom and said, 'Let's go,' " Bardwell recalled.

Brandon Roy was equally incredulous, if not aghast, once his best friend Cole Allen informed him what his brother had just done. Did he really say that to her? Does she think I like her?

"I just wanted my little brother to date girls," Ed Roy explained. "There was not one girl in school he couldn't have dated if he'd tried, but he didn't. I just wanted him to date, and I didn't care who it was."

Brandon Roy had already noticed Tiana Bardwell at school. He also was in no position to pursue her. He didn't want anything to get in the way of basketball. He purposely pushed away all distractions.

"I thought she was cute," he conceded. "But I didn't want him to hook me up."

Of course, this was not the end of it. After virtually no previous contact before the dreaded football-game encounter, Roy and Bardwell ran into each other more and more in the Garfield hallways. They had mutual friends, Bulldogs basketball player Will Conroy in particular. They found themselves in groups of people congregated at school. They started to make small talk. They were no longer strangers. They were gradually at ease in each other's company. Getting acquainted wasn't so unnerving after all for these two, though it went at an agonizingly slow place, over a couple of months. But they still weren't boyfriend and girlfriend.

As Christmas approached, Bardwell, initially shy about interacting with the school's next big basketball star, became impatient and wanted to push for a stronger connection with him. She realized it wasn't going to happen on his end, that he needed some serious prodding. She handed her phone number to Allen and asked him to give it to Roy, along with instructions for Roy to call her over school vacation.

She never heard from Roy. He was busy playing basketball in holiday tournaments. He also was clueless to what was happening around him, that this girl at school had shown a greater interest in him and made a bold move to advance their friendship. Basketball had his attention, nothing else. It didn't register with Roy that Bardwell might react in a negative fashion if he failed to respond to her invitation. There was a certain chilliness awaiting him when classes resumed.

"I didn't know it was serious," Roy pleaded.

"I wouldn't talk to him," Bardwell said.

Slowly, the basketball player figured it out. He also noticed she kept basketball sneakers, purple Converse among them, in her locker, which was intriguing to him. She had dabbled in the game some as a middle-school player, and it brought her a unique nickname—one she wasn't totally enamored with. With multiple hair stylists in her family, she often showed up with a new look. Lardel Sims, a classmate of Bardwell's who later became one of Brandon Roy's closest friends, took notice of the girl's changing hair styles and provided a memorable christening.

"He called me 'Hair Jordan,' " Bardwell said.

Even with a basketball pedigree, Bardwell still had trouble gaining Roy's full attention, as did the rest of the female population at Garfield High. He didn't date. He previously had a casual girlfriend or two in middle school, when dating wasn't really possible, but he hadn't shown much interest in sharing himself with the opposite sex thereafter. There was no shortage of girls vying for his attention. He purposely didn't go there.

"I didn't like dating," Roy said. "I was all about basketball. We were going to the state tournament. I didn't want to mess that up."

"Brandon was in his own world most of the time," said Frances Roy, his grandmother. "He didn't have time for girlfriends."

What happened next was almost as shocking to the entire Roy family as the Bulldogs getting upset by the Foss Falcons twice and not winning a state championship. Brandon offered no clues at all that his social life was about to go through radical change. In fact, he had been more adamant about acquiring a different sort of companion.

"Brandon kept saying, 'Get me a dog, get me a dog,' " his father Tony Roy wisecracked. "I waited too long. He got a girlfriend instead."

Brandon did all of this in a sly manner, which was his preference. He didn't want any input on his social life. He didn't want anyone to know until he was ready to share it. He started visiting his grandmother's house a lot on Beacon Hill, which wasn't all that surprising, considering she was one of his favorite people. Yet there were far more trips than usual. It just so happened that Tiana Bardwell lived on 20th Avenue South, one block from Frances Roy, and Brandon was headed there. Eventually, the rest of the family caught on to this clandestine courtship.

"It was something we had never seen before, with him so shy and wrapped up in basketball," sister Jaamela Roy said. "It was, 'Who is this girl?' He was starting to become this young man in front of me. I didn't have anything against her. But I let him know I didn't like it. I was this jealous little sister. I put my nose up in the air. But Tiana and I would become really close. We became best friends."

At the state tournament, Bardwell finally was introduced to Gina Roy, Brandon's mother. They had spoken on the phone before and now they met in person. This seemed to be a relationship icebreaker for Brandon and Tiana. This young couple didn't get together during the Bulldogs' football season, but the end of basketball season seemed to provide an appropriate opening. Still, the talented guard wasn't nearly as smooth with the way he handled his love life as he was racing up and down the basketball floor.

"I asked her out, or to be my girlfriend, or however that happens," Roy said, stumbling around even more.

Bardwell became the envy of Garfield High, if not thoroughly scorned for this breakthrough. Other girls were jealous and let it show. Girls Tiana regarded as her friends were upset at her and became former friends. She was Brandon Roy's first and only real girlfriend, and they weren't, and they couldn't understand why.

"She wasn't fast like most girls in high school," Roy explained. "She was outspoken, but acted her age. I was a shy guy. I matured slow."

They found they had a lot in common. Neither of their families had a lot of money. Bardwell once wanted a pair of new Jordan sneakers, but couldn't afford them and was a little intimidated by the long line that formed outside the downtown Nike store. Hearing this, Roy, always the saver, grabbed a collection of stray coins he had steadily built up, cashed in about eighty dollars worth of quarters, patiently stood in line for this new line of Jordan footwear, and presented his girlfriend with the shoes she coveted. True love couldn't have been more apparent.

"March 24, 2001," Bardwell said, reciting the day when she and Brandon officially became girlfriend and boyfriend. "We've been together ever since."

"I was the guy you could take home to Dad," Roy said earnestly.

Once the love connection was made and exposed, it actually made sense to everyone in the family. Roy's parents had been virtually inseparable since their middle-school meeting, and the Roy men seemed to know what they wanted in a relationship.

"They weren't the type to have a lot of girlfriends," Frances Roy said. Ed Roy, the football game matchmaker, was satisfied with the outcome. However, he figured his parents were more responsible for leaving an impression that involved lasting love, and his younger brother had bought into it.

"Brandon looks up to my mom a lot," Ed Roy said. "He really has respected my mom forever. She said my dad and her had dated since they were thirteen. I think Brandon respected those morals."

As crazy as it sounds, the *Godfather I* movie, which was far more violent than compassionate, had provided added guidance for Roy in his personal affairs. He watched it over and over. He still watches it. He found a message in this Oscar-winning cinematic epic, one that might surprise everyone.

"He thinks every man has to have a code that he lives by and has to respect himself," Ed Roy said. "I think Brandon really takes that to heart. We used to watch a lot of Mafia movies."

Roy's close friendships usually came with staying power. He met Cole Allen in the sixth grade, in their first year at Hamilton Middle School, perhaps on an outdoor basketball court, though memories are a little hazy going back to preteen years. They became inseparable, particularly at Garfield High. They took the same classes on purpose, heading straight to the counseling office at the start of each quarter if their schedules didn't mesh. They played together in pickup games at lunchtime. They shared in varsity basketball practice after school. Their laid-back personalities made this all work.

"For the longest time, people considered Brandon to be the quiet guy," Allen said. "He would just sit back and observe. That was his trademark."

There was no intrusion on their friendship once Bardwell was added to Roy's world. The three of them regularly hung out together. Allen and Roy used to borrow a tiny Geo Metro car that belonged to Allen's sister and let Bardwell, too young to have a license, drive it while they rode in the back. Allen came up with his own dates so everyone could go to dances and the prom together.

Lardel Sims, who is the same age as Bardwell, was still in middle school when he started showing up at Garfield basketball practices and games. He first met Ed Roy, a senior, and then Brandon Roy, a sophomore, in the gym. Sims was funny and everybody enjoyed his company. He went his own way as an athlete, eventually becoming a Garfield High and Shasta College football player, a fullback. He had a few scrapes at home with a grandfather, and Brandon came through to help him out with emotional and financial support.

On the exterior, Sims and Brandon were sort of an odd couple, this young kid and the budding basketball star. Yet their friendship had no such boundaries related to age or lifestyle, making it permanent.

"We used to sit and talk," Sims said. "He said he saw the same thing in me that I saw in him. He didn't expect me to be on that level."

In high school, these friends gave each other colorful nicknames that haven't been forgotten. Roy was Cleofus and B-Real. Cole was C-40, a takeoff on the rapper E-40. Sims was Cleofus Junior and then Lardelious the Sillious, and Deli for short. Tiana, of course, was Hair Jordan. Allen, Sims, and Bardwell each entered Roy's inner circle, which they found to be mutually exclusive and everlasting. Outside of blood relatives and basketball teammates or hoop acquaintances, it involved only these three people: Brandon's best friend, his next closest friend, and the only person he ever dated. Fear was one reason so few were waved through. Life, while overly kind to Roy in so many ways, kept him guessing otherwise.

"I haven't told anybody this before, but I'm afraid of death," he admitted. "I'm afraid to lose people. That's why I keep a small circle of friends. I try to shelter myself."

Tiana Roy became fully involved in Brandon's world following their uncomfortable introduction at the Garfield High football game. Roy never again let anything get between him and Hair Jordan.

Chapter 7
Early Entry

On a Sunday night, sports department fax machines at the city's two daily newspapers, the *Seattle Post-Intelligencer* and the *Seattle Times*, suddenly started humming and spitting out a one-page press release. Most athletic events were conducted during the afternoon on spring weekends, leaving these places library-quiet and everyone on the sports desks stretching, yawning, and waiting for one week to end and another to start. Sunday evening was always one of the slowest times in the office.

There weren't any sportswriters milling around at the two metro papers on this particular evening, just people systematically designing pages, copy-editing the words turned in, and putting out the next day's edition. Yet once this incoming fax was picked up and read by editors, people were on the phone scurrying to find someone to cover the story.

On May 12, 2002, still a month shy of his Garfield High School graduation, Brandon Roy let his hometown know he had submitted his name for NBA draft early entry. An uncle helped him prepare and distribute the brief statement. Roy had sent a certified letter four days earlier to New York stating his intentions. With a recent change in NCAA rules, aspiring pro-basketball players such as Roy were now permitted to test the market without penalty. They could work out for NBA teams without forfeiting their amateur standing to find out where they stood, and return to college if they were in over their heads or not satisfied with their draft assessment. They could backtrack, providing they didn't sign with a sports agent or accept any workout expenses other than participating in the NBA-sponsored, pre-draft camp in Chicago a few weeks before the draft.

Still, this was surprising news. Just a month earlier, Roy had said he likely would honor the University of Washington basketball scholarship he had accepted, even with the firing of the coach who had signed him and made him feel wanted, Bob Bender, and having to play for a new guy coming in, Lorenzo Romar. Bender was let go following a third consecutive losing season, with the Huskies athletic department becoming too impatient to let the coach have another year to try and turn things around with Roy on the roster.

This looked like a huge setback out of the gates for Romar, a former Washington point guard who left his Saint Louis University coaching job to assume control of a program coming off three consecutive losing seasons, most recently an 11-18 disaster during the 2001-02 schedule. But the new coach didn't view Roy's actions as a negative or foregone conclusion, which was one of Romar's strengths. He would wait out the process and see what happened.

"It was a unique situation of circumstances," Romar reasoned. "If they told him, 'You're a first-round draft choice,' he would have looked into it for two reasons: first, he could, and second, he had not qualified [academically] and this might be an easy way out. I never thought once that this was some arrogant, cocky kid who was reaching for the NBA. It was sort of an experiment."

The University of Washington, even with Bender's program falling into a precarious state, had won a significant recruiting battle with the University of Arizona and Gonzaga University for Roy's services. The Zags, four years into an unimagined basketball upgrade that had provided them with continuous national attention, put Roy on the forty-five-minute flight to Spokane and brought him over for a campus visit. But Gonzaga never really stood a chance with him; nothing clicked between the player and the West Coast Conference program.

"He kind of looked around and held his nose up at us," Gonzaga coach Mark Few said, indignantly recounting the recruiting visit in his office. "It wasn't Seattle."

That's not how Roy remembers it. He thought he was polite and respectful throughout the recruiting visit, though he didn't really want to take the trip in the first place. He already knew where he wanted to go. He preferred to stay home and play for the Huskies and Bender. He only agreed to come over to check out Few, a college coach with a burgeoning reputation, because he had heard good things about the man. However, Roy was turned off when he arrived in the state's second-largest city. The Gonzaga coaching staff sat him down and proceeded to bad-mouth the Washington program, rather than promote what the Zags had to offer.

"That sort of backfired on them," Roy said. "They made Washington look bad. I felt I had to go help and defend Washington now. I flew back to Seattle, and it was never more clear about what I wanted to do."

A much more serious challenger for Roy's basketball talents came from Arizona. The regal Wildcats coach Lute Olson, someone former Washington coach Marv Harshman once likened to "an English Lord," usually could descend on Seattle, or any West Coast city, charm any big-time local recruit he wanted, and take him back to the desert without much opposition.

In 1994, Olson literally stole Franklin High School guard Jason Terry away from the Huskies in the eleventh hour of recruiting. This happened even after the kid had been spurned earlier by Olson and the Wildcats in favor of another recruit who would back out, and Terry had offered a verbal commitment to Bender's coaching staff while sitting alongside fellow Washington recruit Donald Watts in a televised news conference in Seattle. Terry had once worked at Huskies games during high school as a popcorn vendor, so he knew his way around their arena.

The year before Terry's services were secured, Arizona had signed Decatur High School forward Michael Dickerson, a widely pursued prospect in suburban Federal Way who was unsuccessfully courted by Washington State coach Kelvin Sampson, a persuasive man on the recruiting front even back then.

Roy, however, said no thanks to Olson. It wasn't an easy thing to do. Arizona put on its usual recruiting full-court press. On the first day high-school players were eligible for college coaching contacts as juniors, Roy took a phone call from USC first and then Arizona. Thereafter, he spoke with persistent Wildcats assistant coach Rodney Tention once a week, the two usually chatting from forty-five minutes to an hour. Roy's initial reaction to this recruiting connection was one of typical teenage awe.

"It was like, 'Oh, wow, it's Arizona,' " Roy recalled. "Other coaches would call and ask me who had called and I said Arizona and they went, 'Oh, wow,' and kind of shied away. I thought, 'I've got Arizona, I don't need any other calls. If I've got a call from Arizona, I must be one of the top players in the country.' "

Olson and his assistant coaches put great effort into signing three players that year who could have given Arizona one of its most celebrated recruiting classes. At one point, they felt confident about gaining a commitment from each one. Targeted were Hassan Adams, Andre Iguodala, and Roy, all players the Arizona staff had projected for NBA careers, which is exactly where each landed. Privately, these coaches considered Roy the most gifted of the trio. Publicly, they made a big run at him. In the end, the Wildcats went two-for-three, missing out on the Seattle kid.

The first moment of truth for Roy came in October 2001, when Olson arrived in Seattle for an in-home visit, presumably to close the deal. His presence at Garfield High had the basketball-minded school all abuzz. The impressionable Roy and the white-haired, immaculately dressed Arizona basketball coach strolled through the halls together. Olson reached out to the player's giddy Bulldogs teammates and classmates in a polite, friendly manner, shaking hands right and left. A Jimi Hendrix sighting at this, the renowned and deceased rock star's former high school, couldn't have caused more of a commotion.

"He was a legendary coach and he was standing in the Garfield hallways and walking around with us," said Cole Allen, a Bulldogs guard and Roy's best friend. "We were flabbergasted. It was really cool. I don't recall telling Brandon personally to go to Arizona, but I remember people generally talking and the consensus was Arizona puts out more pros. People were saying Washington hasn't put anybody into the NBA. Washington was at the bottom of the barrel. Washington wasn't anything then. People said, 'If you turn down Lute Olson, you're crazy.' "

For a frank, private discussion, Roy, his father, and Arizona's Olson and Tention drove to Frances Roy's nearby home on Beacon Hill. During Brandon's recruitment, Grandma Roy also had hosted the University of Oregon's Ernie Kent, Boston College's Al Skinner, Bender, and Few in her front room. Later, she received a card in the mail from Few thanking her for her hospitality. With Olson, the conversation began with academics and then steered toward the Wildcats basketball program. Tony Roy pointedly asked the basketball coach, now well past retirement age, how long he planned to stay at Arizona. As long as he was healthy, Olson responded without hesitation.

Brandon Roy admitted to the Wildcats coaches he was leaning toward staying home. He wanted to play for Washington and Bender. He wanted his family to see him play and help turn those woebegone Huskies around. Undeterred, Olson said he still would love to have Roy play for the Wildcats, but would respect whatever decision the player made. The coach had been through this before. He knew he wasn't out of the running with Roy. He was still working this five-star recruit, using his charisma. It apparently was working, too.

"I kind of wanted to tell him I'd go there," Roy admitted. "At the time, they might have had me."

The second moment of truth for Roy involved his Arizona campus recruiting visit. Olson asked him to come on an upcoming November weekend when the Wildcats hosted the University of Kansas. That way, Roy would be fully exposed to a supercharged college basketball environment in Tucson with all of the big-game trappings. He could see two top-ten teams going at it in front of a rollicking full house at McKale Center with national TV cameras recording everything. The hope was he would get so wrapped up in all of the hype and excitement that he wouldn't be able to reject the school's advances. Roy knew this. He canceled the trip.

"In the back of my mind, I thought if I take this visit, I'm pretty sure I'm going to sign with them," Roy recalled. "I couldn't tell them no. I was scared, so I decided I was going to pass on my visit."

"I was shocked when he turned Olson down," said Dave Belmonte, one of Roy's Garfield assistant coaches and a former Franklin head coach. "That was like turning down God."

"Washington was not a bad choice, but my opinion was he should have gone to Arizona," Garfield coach Wayne Floyd said.

Arizona followers naturally were surprised by Roy's decision. So were people in Seattle. This was Olson's first swing and a miss at a Northwest kid, and this one was supposed to be as good, if not better, than the others. Was there finally a crack in the recruiting wall of this college basketball empire? Was it something the English Lord said or didn't say? With the Seattle market a tough sell for the first time, there no doubt was some deep soul-searching done by this veteran Wildcats coaching staff after this recruiting class had sorted itself out.

"We were disappointed," Olson said. "We recruited Brandon hard. We really liked him as a kid and a player. We felt we would be a good spot for him. At one point, I think we felt we were in pretty good shape. But recruiting is like that. You never know until the end what's going to happen."

Roy found the same thing to be true in obtaining a qualifying Scholastic Aptitude Test score. He still didn't have one. He actually wasn't in any position to attend Washington, let alone listen to Arizona's persuasive advances. Roy was concerned he might end up at a faraway junior college, same as his brother Ed. He was worried he might never be heard from again as a basketball player, which is what happened to his older sibling.

At this point, Roy determined he would audition for the pros. Jamal Crawford, then a second-year Chicago Bulls guard and his good friend, encouraged Roy to give NBA early entry a try. What could it hurt? Crawford had left for the league after one turbulent and abbreviated season at the University of Michigan—his college eligibility challenged over his relationship with a Seattle businessman amid allegations that Crawford had received extra benefits. Crawford was forced to turn pro, and it had worked out for him. Former Sonics coach Bob Hopkins was another who weighed in and told Roy there was no harm in giving the pros a try.

There were many unsolicited voices of reason, too. Garfield High teammate Alex Hatzey, Sonics coach Nate McMillan, and Franklin High alumnus and then-Atlanta Hawks guard Jason Terry were among those who suggested he consider passing on early entry. Hatzey offered his opinion to Roy after spotting him in the gym one day and asking him if he was indeed serious about testing the NBA. McMillan shared his concern with Floyd that Roy was taking on too much too soon, and Floyd delivered this message. Terry likewise encountered Roy in the gym.

"I told him, 'I think you could play in the NBA, but I don't think you can play in the NBA right now,' " Hatzey said.

"I just felt he should go to college," recalled McMillan, who later became Roy's pro coach.

"He went to college, which I encouraged," said Terry, who eventually found himself guarding his friend in the pros.

Roy wasn't averse to second opinions. Even with all the unsolicited feedback, he sought one out on his own. He went to his beloved grandmother and asked her what she thought about him taking this bold step. Her input carried a lot of weight. The grandson received an answer that probably didn't surprise him.

"I told him, 'Listen, hon, that's a decision you have to make yourself. I know you're hearing all sorts of things. You are the one who has to live with it,' " said Frances Roy, whose solutions for dealing with tough situations always had leaned to the spiritual side. "I just pray on stuff and leave it alone. I just act on faith."

Considering the Roy family history, this wasn't such a radical move. When she was eighteen, Frances Roy had hopped on a bus alone in Louisiana and headed for Los Angeles to start a new life. When he was eighteen, Tony Roy left home and joined the Marines, figuring that this was the best way to care for his pregnant girlfriend soon to be his wife. Now here was seventeen-year-old Brandon Roy acting similarly bold and adventuresome at such a young age, trying to make something substantial happen in his world.

Over the next month, Roy talked to NBA teams in Portland, Miami, San Antonio, and Toronto. For financial reasons, he worked out only for the Trail Blazers, traveling to their practice facility south of Portland accompanied by his father and one of his father's friends. For two grueling hours, Roy was treated to a fairly comprehensive basketball inspection by the

Trail Blazers front office, which included general manager John Nash, the director of player personnel, and assistant coaches, all people no longer affiliated with the NBA franchise.

Roy was matched up against six-foot-eight free-agent forward Boris Diaw, a French professional player two years older and three inches taller than Roy who was seeking a pro-basketball job and wouldn't land one with the Trail Blazers. Roy played one-on-one games against the more aggressive, more muscled European forward who didn't speak any English at the time. The teenager was asked to run the floor repeatedly to demonstrate how well he could push the basketball. He was put through a gut-check workout that honestly told him all he needed to know about his pro chances at that moment.

"I said, 'Whoa, that was tough,' " Roy recalled. "I wasn't physically ready to go that hard at that level yet. I was honest with myself."

Eight years later, Diaw, a starting forward for the Charlotte Bobcats, vaguely remembered his time auditioning in the Pacific Northwest, only that he was matched up against some kid, who was unknown to him. Diaw was outwardly surprised when informed who his workout partner was that day.

"I didn't know that was Brandon Roy," Diaw professed, his eyes getting bigger and a wide smile forming after hearing this. "I just remember it was a kid, and the workout was long. We went one-one-one for a couple of hours. At that point, I didn't think he was ready. He was just coming out of high school. But I didn't know that was Brandon Roy. You have told me something I didn't know."

The Trail Blazers were prepared to readily discourage Roy's NBA pursuits if he hadn't received that message on his own. A file on Roy's 2002 workout was prepared by the front-office staff and kept in a drawer for future team executives. Roy's overall talent assessment from that Portland staff was not kind. There were questions about his conditioning and pace of play. The Trail Blazers' negative take on Roy back then was ironic considering their future dependence on him.

"I should keep silent," Trail Blazers general manager Kevin Pritchard said. "They weren't very high on him."

Toronto called next and invited Roy to a four-player workout. The University of Oregon's Freddie Jones, University of Missouri's Kareem Rush, and early-entry hopeful Lenny Cooke, a schoolboy legend from New York, were the others summoned to come north and show what they had. The Miami Heat also asked Roy to travel across the country for a workout. At this juncture, he had to make a decision whether to continue with this process or abort it. It all boiled down to finances, and he didn't have them. Potential NBA prospects had to pay for their airline tickets and hotel rooms in case they wanted to retain their amateur standing. On short notice, these expenses wouldn't come cheaply.

Roy and his parents determined they couldn't afford more pro basketball inspections. They declined all further workout offers from NBA teams. A final insult came when Roy wasn't one of the fifty players invited by league officials to the Chicago pre-draft camp, an early June gathering sponsored by the NBA, one in which all participants' travel and lodging expenses were picked up by the league, and no one's amateur standing was threatened. It was humbling to be rejected. Roy called the league office to ask why he was omitted and didn't receive an explanation.

Outside of his basketball ego getting bruised slightly during the process, Roy felt his early sampling of NBA life was well worth the trouble. He didn't think he was far off from playing with the big boys. He was convinced more than ever he was going to be a pro soon enough.

"I felt that I could play in the NBA one day," he said. "I just had to get stronger. My skill level was there. Everything was there. I decided playing at a high level for a long time was something I could learn in college."

Roy had given the pros his best shot as a skinny kid who would grow into an NBA body. Irked Seattle basketball fans blamed Washington and its coaching instability for this prized player giving early entry any consideration at all. Chances are Roy would have tried it anyway, regardless of whether Bender or Romar held the Huskies' top job. His grades weren't in good shape, forcing him to consider his alternatives. He had confidence in his game, giving him big ideas. In the end, he was bold enough to try it, though he made a ready promise to his father in advance that he would join the Washington basketball program and play for Romar if his initial involvement with the pros didn't pan out.

"Brandon was never sheltered," said Bender, who still spoke with Roy after the coach lost his college job. "He had the ability to understand the big picture. He was mature. I told Brandon to go to Washington and do what he expected to do there."

A few days after the 2001-02 basketball season ended for the Huskies and five months after receiving a signed letter of intent from Brandon Roy, Bender was called in and fired by Washington athletic director Barbara Hedges. She was encouraged by leading boosters to pull the plug on the nine-year coach, though she insisted that the decision was all hers. In the aftermath, Roy fielded calls at home and said he was disappointed at the coaching change but would wait and see who the new Huskies coach was before deciding his next move.

There remained a very good chance Bender would have remained the Washington basketball coach had Hedges been just a little more patient, if not deaf to her donors' demands, and allowed Bender to welcome Roy into the program and revitalize it. Roy was the kind of player who could make any college basketball coach look good, and everyone knew it. Otherwise Lute Olson and Mark Few wouldn't have shown up in person at his high school or grandmother's house, or both. Bender just happened to get there first. It just wasn't soon enough for him to keep his Huskies coaching job.

"We were the one program that really believed in him from the start," Bender said of his most prized Washington recruit. "I wouldn't say I was shortchanged, but I was disappointed. Things happen. I would have liked the chance to coach him."

Chapter 8
The Container Yard

Behind the chain-link fence, abandoned rail line, trailer-shaped office building, beeping forklifts, stacks and stacks of colored shipping containers, and three rows of idling trucks parked six to eight deep, a crude basketball hoop was attached to a blue metal column. At Northwest Container Services, this sagging rim couldn't have been more out of place. The same was true for Brandon Roy.

For seven months ending in January 2003, from 8 A.M. to 1 P.M., five days per week, and for $10.95 an hour, Roy worked at this dirty, dusty place at 6110 West Marginal Way Southwest, two industrial yards over from the west bank of Seattle's Duwamish River.

This was where Roy was forced into exile from college basketball once the NCAA Clearinghouse started playing fast and loose with his Scholastic Aptitude Test scores, keeping him from enrolling on time at the University of Washington, and keeping him in limbo. His mom often dropped him off for his early morning shift.

"All my friends were moving on," Roy said. "I was working at the docks."

His job exposed him to plenty of nauseating and humbling duties. A yard supervisor made Roy sweep mindlessly over a cement area that couldn't possibly have needed more attention, just to see how this big-time college basketball recruit would respond; the man in charge finally warmed up to Roy after all of his attempts failed to draw a negative reaction.

Roy operated forklifts, handled truck dispatching, and emptied garbage containers. His worst chore, however, was climbing inside the twenty-foot containers with a co-worker to pressure-wash them, especially after the metal boxes were used to transport cowhides, known as hide-liners, to slaughterhouses. This exercise involved wearing a protective mask. Everyone else nearby on the work site was forced to hold their nose. The odors emanating from these crates smelled so foul from the bovine carcasses that they filtered through the entire yard. Salmon shipments were a little kinder, leaving more tolerable fish guts and oils to clean up with a less pungent, yet still unpleasant, smell.

Northwest Container Services was responsible for cleaning, repairing, and restoring these boxes used for global shipping. Fourteen employees kept everything in the yard moving. Scholarship athletes such as Roy were used to supplement the work crew until attorney Rich Padden, a University of Washington alumnus and part owner, sold his interest in the business.

Roy was a well-liked employee because he did everything he was asked with a stoic expression and a sense of responsibility. While other Huskies football and basketball players had demonstrated considerable ego and little interest in the job that needed to be done, Roy went to work.

"He was down to earth," said Bob Sherwood, Northwest Container Services district manager and a short, hyper man with spiky hair. "You could sense from the other guys that Rich had sent us that he didn't have the same attitude. Everybody knew he was going to make the NBA. I even asked Brandon what he going to do when he had to go one-on-one with Kobe Bryant? He just shook his head and said, 'I don't know.' "

Padden took an interest in inner-city Seattle kids such as Roy, encouraging them to take education seriously and offering them pro-bono legal advice, particularly those from low-income families. His intentions were honorable, nothing more. He didn't want the aspiring pro athletes among them getting ripped off either. A case in point was Martell Webster, who ended up going straight from Seattle Preparatory School to the NBA, bypassing a Washington scholarship in the process. Webster was misled, signing an obscure document with them that unknowingly removed his college option, and he needed help finding a different management group he could trust.

Padden helped Roy obtain a tutor to prepare for the Scholastic Aptitude Test, mandatory for college admittance. He encouraged Roy to take a stronger interest in the classroom and keep all options open. Padden wasn't shy about offering his opinion, and it was well received.

"He didn't care how good I was at basketball," Roy said. "He demanded that you be good at school, too."

Amid all of the intense industrial activity, Northwest Container Services kept a basketball hoop propped up in the back on the corner of a rusted repair shop. Stacked truck tires, a strewn water hose, and loose gravel served as dribbling obstacles. A barbed-wire fence that lined the back of the yard and several exposed nails sticking out of loose boards were added punishment for anyone who veered off course when attacking the rim.

Roy was careful not to enter the lunchtime pickup games and risk needless injury. It was safe enough for him to play games of "twenty-one," a laid-back competition that involved making matching shots with no physical contact. Roy took part maybe ten times, to the delight of the blue-collar workers on the job. There were laughs when shop supervisor Rudy "Woody" Sandoval, an extra-short five-foot-one man with a shaved head who had played point guard for south Seattle's Evergreen and Highline high schools, tried to steal the ball from Roy and unintentionally ran through his legs.

"Anything you told him to do, all the grunt work, he did it," Sandoval said of Roy. "He was a hard worker. Out of the other guys that came here, he was the hardest worker we had. I actually told him that he was going to go to the NBA and he did that. I'm really proud of him."

Roy returned to the shipping-container yard during the summer of his first pro basketball offseason in 2007 with a camera crew and Portland Trail Blazers media liaison to document his previous hardscrabble existence for the NBA TV network. This was so different from Mom dropping him off and picking him up later. Roy also was quizzed about the industrial company while doing a guest spot on Fox TV's irreverent *Best Damn Sports Show*; he good-naturedly got out of his chair and pretended to clean the camera lens to demonstrate his blue-collar capabilities.

"I laughed at that," Sherwood said. "He was such a great kid. You don't see that too often. He really interacted well with all the guys."

Way before the pros, Roy had to scramble to make college basketball happen. He signed new scholarship letter-of-intent documents with Washington after his brief foray with NBA early entry. He became better acquainted with the Huskies' new coach Lorenzo Romar, eventually building a trusting relationship. There was still an adjustment period, and he needed to prove himself all over again.

"I thought he was a great player," said Bob Bender, his previous coach. "The skills were there at an early age. The blueprint was there. Good family. Good program. There were guys who could score, but didn't know how to play offense. He made passes. He knew how to play offense. That was a sign of someone who knows the game."

"Me and Bender had a really good relationship," Roy said. "He came to a lot of my high-school games. I was excited to play for him. He saw my game and he understood how I played."

Roy talked with Romar for the first time by phone the night after the coach was introduced as a new hire at a combination news conference and pep rally at Washington's Edmundson Pavilion. They met in person two days later. They chatted easily and got acquainted. Romar was more personable and relaxed than Roy had expected; the teenager felt like they had known each other for a long time. Romar likewise was impressed with this tall, skinny teenager who demonstrated no pretenses or inflated self-worth.

The Huskies coach knew all about Roy's widespread reputation, but didn't catch his first glimpse of him in action on the court until a few weeks later, when Roy participated in a tournament for selected high school seniors at Seattle University. Romar's immediate impression was favorable. Leaving the Redhawks' gym early to fulfill another commitment as the new Washington basketball coach, Romar told Roy's father with a straight face, "I think we're going to be all right with Brandon."

There was still the matter of that nagging test score. Roy couldn't play college basketball without it. He was a bright kid but because he hadn't fared well as a student, closing this gap was going to be difficult. He failed three times to obtain the minimum SAT score required to proceed with college. The NCAA Clearinghouse in Indianapolis even lost one of his tests, prompting an exchange of nasty letters through attorneys from both sides.

Questioned over the paperwork slipup, the NCAA responded in a cryptic manner that junior college was an option Roy might want to consider.

Roy took the test again and improved by three hundred points, the result of regular meetings with his personal tutor. It also was such a healthy jump that automatic red flags went up, prompting yet another review from the NCAA Clearinghouse. Roy needed to match or surpass a 930 result, and he did that. It still wasn't enough. The NCAA rejected his test with the insinuation that he was a cheater. He was more stunned and disappointed with the outcome than angry. Others were offended by what seemed a totally arbitrary decision.

"I was so upset when they said he cheated on his SAT," said Jenni Maughan-MacDonald, the Garfield teacher who tutored Roy. "I knew he wasn't that kind of kid."

"I didn't want people to think I was a cheater," Roy said.

Where Roy once felt he had all kinds of basketball options available to him, he now was starting to think he had none. This was never more obvious than in his despondent July 2002 phone call to Romar, who was on the road recruiting at the time. The coach had to pull over his rental car to the side of the road and spend several minutes calming Roy. They talked at length over what needed to be done. It all seemed so daunting to Roy, who was close to giving in. "He was thinking, 'Forget it, school may not be for me,' " Romar said. "That was a down time."

It got worse before it got better. Washington classes started in late September without Roy. Huskies basketball practice started in the middle of October without Roy. The regular-season games started in late November. And so did Pac-10 play in early January. Roy chose to sit with his dad in the uppermost seats at Edmundson Pavilion, where nobody recognized him and he could watch the games without anyone hounding him about his uncertain status. He hung out at practice, able to watch but not participate, and even that was hard.

Getting over his blue mood, Roy was determined to make something positive happen. It was decided he should aim for winter quarter to get eligible and remove some of the pressure he was feeling. He took the SAT a fourth time to satisfy the NCAA Clearinghouse, forced to fill out the exam at rival Franklin High School, no less. He understood the high stakes better than ever now. His immediate basketball future depended on the outcome.

"This is my life, and it is either two years at junior college or the University of Washington,' " Roy said a few days prior to the Saturday testing.

While everyone else was in school, Roy kept busy. Besides working each morning at Northwest Container Services, he studied four times per week near the University District with a University of Washington senior who was his tutor. He was put through nightly basketball workouts by his AAU coach, Lou Hobson, in the Wychoff Gymnasium at Saint Joseph's church, often accompanied by his father. His girlfriend, Tiana, was a Garfield junior, leaving Brandon and her little time to see each other. It wasn't an easy existence.

"He said it was the loneliest time in his life," Hobson said.

Yet Roy found lots of company whenever he was at Saint Joe's, a popular hoop hangout favored by the city's best players because of its centralized location. You never knew who was going to come through the door and pick up a basketball and start bouncing it. One night, Roy fired up shots alongside Jordan Schultz, a University Prep School player and son of Starbucks chairman and chief executive officer and then-Sonics owner Howard Schultz. That same evening, former NBA and Seattle University standout Eddie Miles, nicknamed "The Man with the Golden Arm," and his son Troy Miles, a former University of Nevada player, wandered in and sat down. A high-school girl took shots at a side basket while her father supervised and her mom sat in the stands and read a magazine. On this day, the slender yet graceful Roy wore a sleeveless yellow shirt, red and white shorts, and black high-top sneakers. He worked out diligently, running through a standard set of drills, all under the close supervision of Hobson.

The AAU coach, however, was not happy at all when I—a *Seattle Post-Intelligencer* sportswriter—and one of the newspaper's photographers showed up at Saint Joe's for a prearranged interview and photo shoot with Roy and his father. Hobson huddled with Tony Roy in the bleachers and could be heard voicing strong objections. The coach backed off once he was convinced we were there to do a tactful update on the idle player, not to trash him. Brandon was pleased his daily routine was still considered newsworthy. It made him feel wanted again, and Brandon, in ensuing years, would make it a point to remind me of the good feelings generated by the interview that night.

"Everybody was scared," Brandon said. "Lou was so protective and he said, 'I don't want them to write anything negative about you.' I was kind of the forgotten guy then, so I was glad that someone was still interested in me."

With his grades keeping him from enrolling right away at Washington, Roy was officially a college basketball free agent once more. Schools such as the University of Arizona and University of Kansas wanted to see if he finally was willing to relocate. However, he intended to stay loyal to Romar, just as he had done with Hobson on the AAU circuit. The eighteen-year-old was eager to get started with the Huskies. He dreamed about becoming a top-five lottery pick, though he wasn't sure if or when that would happen. All that mattered was that SAT score.

On January 16, 2003, Roy finally was ruled eligible hours before a Washington-California basketball game at Edmundson Pavilion. His fourth test score was approved after taking nearly two months to pass through the red tape in Indianapolis.

Impatient for an answer, Roy sought out Romar, who looked down and feigned sadness. "I said, 'I didn't get it, did I?' " Brandon said, before catching on. "He said, 'No, I'm just trying to figure out how to get you a uniform tonight.' We hugged for five minutes."

In anticipation of achieving a positive result, Roy had audited UW classes once winter quarter began, so he wasn't too far behind when he officially enrolled in school that day. He missed the team's first fourteen games and wasn't in great playing shape. He pulled on a uniform for the game against the Golden Bears and sat on the bench, but didn't play. He had a lot to learn about the team before he would take the floor. He repeatedly quizzed Anthony Washington, his Garfield High School and now college teammate, about the nuances of Division I basketball. The Huskies could have used him that night, losing 73-66.

Everyone was overjoyed for Roy. Getting into college was a huge accomplishment for him and the entire family. His younger sister Jaamela admittedly wasn't ready to see him head to Washington, purely for selfish reasons. The family's practical joker and pickup-game partner was headed out the door and getting on with his life, and it was going to be an adjustment for everyone.

"He moved out for college and I was so sad," Jaamela Roy said. "He was just going to the U-Dub, but it was like the end of the world for me. I wrote him letters telling him that I didn't want things to ever end. We'd been through so much together."

Two days after officially becoming a college student and basketball player, Roy received enthusiastic applause when he was inserted during each half of the Huskies' game against Stanford University. He took a three-pointer that missed. He drew a questionable foul call. Playing just five minutes, he contributed four assists and two rebounds in a 73-68 victory over the Cardinal. He was 1-0 as a college player.

The day he became eligible, Roy learned the Washington offense in just forty-five minutes in the east practice gym at Edmundson Pavilion, showing off his basketball intelligence. Two months into the season, other Huskies players still didn't know Romar's offensive system and probably never would. "The day Brandon became eligible was the day he became our best player," the coach said.

Romar had patiently waited for Roy to have his flirtation with the NBA and overcome the lingering test-score obstacle. Getting this top-notch player into school was his coaching reward. Roy was someone he could build his Pac-10 program around. This was someone who could turn the Huskies into instant and consistent winners. Roy had demonstrated how determined he was to get into school and play basketball for Washington. He had been rejected and humbled and tested. Motivation would never be a question with this player. "I overcame the hardest thing I ever had to overcome in my life," Roy said.

That included climbing through and cleaning out those rancid shipping containers.

Chapter 9
A Huskies Revival

Washington basketball players quickly learned their new teammate had a unique set of offensive moves. The "bailout" was his best one. With it, freshman swingman Brandon Roy performed a subtle spin maneuver to lose his defender, used his ambidextrous ability to make anyone else in his way look silly, and scored a clever basket easily with either hand.

Roy also was good at losing everyone when it came to crowded elevators. They made him claustrophobic. They made him uncomfortable to the point he would rather walk up thirty flights of hotel stairs than squeeze in.

"Whenever we were traveling, there would be people on the elevators and he'd say, 'This elevator is packed, I'll get on another one,' " Huskies coach Lorenzo Romar said. "After seeing this so many times, I asked him, 'Brandon, do you have an aversion to elevators?' "

Friends and teammates thought this was all very funny. On a trip to play in a three-on-three street basketball tournament in Vancouver, British Columbia, Roy allowed himself to step into a hotel elevator with his buddies. He might have been okay on this ride if one of them wasn't Will Conroy. Aware of Roy's phobia, Conroy impishly started jumping up and down on the moving elevator. He made it stall between floors. Conroy made his friend cringe.

"He was looking at the wall like his life was over," Conroy recalled.

"I wanted to kill him," Roy confirmed.

Roy sat down, trying not to panic, muttering to himself. He reached for the emergency elevator phone and called for help. A woman on the other end wasn't all that sympathetic. She scolded Roy and said he and his friends shouldn't have been jumping up and down. She also said an elevator repairman wouldn't reach them for an hour. Roy hung up and then called her right back, his anxiety starting to spiral out of control in the close quarters.

"I said, 'My friend doesn't look good. He looks like he's going to pass out,' " Roy said. He was describing himself, but, in a bit of comeuppance, he also was describing his good friend Conroy. "Will is claustrophobic now, and getting all sweaty and hot, and he calls and they said it would be only a half hour. I just said, 'I'm not taking any more elevators.' "

Unwilling to wait for help to arrive, Roy pried open the door to the car, saw that they were between floors and that everyone needed to jump down only a few feet to get off, and he led an exodus out.

Even alone, Roy has had his moments of elevator angst. On a road trip to Stanford University, he walked onto a hotel service elevator, thinking it looked nice enough inside, plus he had it all to himself. The door closed and nothing happened. He needed a key to ride this car anywhere. He also needed a key just to get the door back open and get out. He picked up the emergency phone and sought help.

"Coach Romar was standing at the front desk when I called and he thought it was funny," Roy said.

Two games into his college career, Roy had a lot to learn about Division I basketball. After losing at the University of Oregon, 91-66, the freshman was summoned to Romar's hotel room for a film critique. Chances are he took the stairs to get there. There still were plenty of other adjustments for Roy to make—pleasing his coach was one of them. The assessment of his play against the Ducks was brutal.

Even after his painstaking struggle to become academically eligible, Roy, who had asked to play the final thirteen games rather than sit out with a redshirt season, wasn't going to be treated gingerly by his head coach. Roy was informed that he was out of position here and had screwed up there in the blowout loss.

"This was my second game on the team and he's already yelling at me," Roy recalled. "He said, 'Remember, you wanted to play.' It was, 'Man, is this guy hard or what?' But he wanted what was best for me. Ever since I walked out of that room that day, I was okay. I knew what was expected. I couldn't feel sorry for myself. What was I going do? Say I didn't want to play now because it was too hard?"

"He needed a push," Romar said. "Brandon was so smooth, like a Jamaal Wilkes. It looked like he wasn't trying. There were times he didn't push himself early in his career."

Sharing the floor with Huskies forward Doug Wrenn was another delicate matter for Roy. The former O'Dea High School standout began his college career at the University of Connecticut, started a couple of games as a freshman, and was asked to leave the Big East school when he couldn't stay out of trouble, in one case shoplifting some basketball shoes. Desperate to right his slumping Washington program, coach Bob Bender not only took a big gamble on Wrenn but built his final team around him and watched the Huskies slip to 11-18, costing him his nine-year job. Wrenn was tossed from practice one day, bad-mouthing his coaches as he left the gym, after he purposely elbowed teammate Errol Knight in the face, one reason Knight later transferred to Gonzaga University.

Roy idolized Wrenn, who was four years older, when Wrenn was the highest-recruited high school player in Seattle in 1998. Roy looked forward to lining up beside him on the college level. However, Wrenn, who led the Huskies in scoring with a 19.5 average, was named to the All-Pac-10 first team and selected conference newcomer of the year under Bender's guidance, wasn't nearly unselfish enough to satisfy Romar.

With two games left in Los Angeles, Romar replaced Wrenn in the starting lineup with Roy, sending a message to both players. One was on his way out, eventually told he wouldn't be allowed to return for his senior season, making him zero-for-two with Division I college programs; the other was eased into a starting spot because he had shown he deserved a full-time role. Roy progressed quickly. He averaged 13.7 points per game over his final four outings. The value of these two players was fairly obvious to

Romar after the coach was left with a trying 10-17 first season. Wrenn had to go; Roy was a building block. There was proof.

"On our highlight video that year, there was a play where Brandon could have shot the ball, but he passed it to Doug, who scored," Romar pointed out. "Brandon stares at Doug as they run up the floor, looking for something. He wants acknowledgement for a good pass, that they're teammates, something, and he didn't get it. I'm ninety percent sure that's what he was thinking. Brandon would have loved for it to work with Doug. But he didn't get that acknowledgement."

Wrenn had tested Romar's patience throughout the previous season. He was benched at the end of their first game together, a season-opening loss to Montana State University at home, for not following directions and was lectured in front of everyone in the arena. He was temporarily dropped from the starting lineup for missing curfew on the Oregon road trip, finding Romar sitting in the lobby and waiting for him to return, with a Bible open in the coach's lap. Once cast adrift, Wrenn took his game overseas and then played for the minor-league Kansas City Knights of the American Basketball Association. He ended up in prison years later for a suburban Seattle road-rage incident, after angrily waving a gun at another motorist. First it was a basketball, now he was unable to share the street.

Roy wore jersey No. 3 for the Huskies, one digit lower than he'd answered to during much of his Garfield career. Huskies teammate Jeffrey Day already had claimed No. 4, so Roy had to find something different from the number he wore for most of his high-school career. His alternative college selection was symbolic—he chose his brother's number. Brandon took that jersey to pay homage to his big brother.

"He went through some complications with college and didn't get a chance to play," the younger Roy said. "I told him, 'When I get there I'm going to wear your number.' "

"I think it was a great honor that he showed the way he felt about me," Ed Roy said.

After Doug Wrenn was gone, Romar turned the Washington basketball team over to Brandon Roy and Nate Robinson, those fifth-grade buddies from Rainier View Elementary finally reunited. As freshmen, they both were late additions for the Huskies. While Roy waited to get his grades approved and missed those first fourteen games, Robinson entered school as a football player, same as his father, and became a starting defensive back for a Sun Bowl-bound team. Because of his postseason trip to El Paso, Texas, Robinson was five games late in reporting to the Huskies as a walk-on player for the basketball season.

Roy was a super glider, Robinson all shocks and struts. They were teammates, classmates, and road roommates. They probably talked incessantly about playing in the NBA again, but no longer faced chalkboard detention. Edmundson Pavilion now was their playground.

Romar often put four or five freshmen on the floor together near the end of that first year with the Huskies just to see what would happen. It made everyone dream a little. Consecutive overtime losses at home to the University of Arizona and Arizona State University by a combined five points demonstrated to everyone, namely that these confident, young basketball players including Roy and Robinson, could compete at a high level, that good things were coming some day.

"We can be the Fab Five at Washington, with me, Brandon, Bobby Jones, Mike Jensen, and Anthony Washington," Robinson said boldly after the Arizona defeat.

Roy's freshman season ended with an 83-72 defeat at UCLA, preventing the Huskies from qualifying for the recently reinstated Pac-10 Tournament. With only the top eight teams advancing at the time, they finished ninth and stayed home. Roy went back to Seattle impressed with Pauley Pavilion, but insulted by Bruins coach Steve Lavin, who had been an inadvertent heckler on the sideline and was fired by UCLA a short time later for his overall coaching shortcomings.

"I remember Lavin saying to his players, 'Roy can't shoot, so back up,' " he said. "I heard it. I also heard that I couldn't shoot free throws, either. So I worked hard on all of those things in the summer. I listened to all the things those coaches were saying on the sideline to me."

When he wasn't polishing his game, these were simple times for the future NBA player. After living in a campus dormitory as required of all freshman, Roy moved back to his West Seattle home and resided there throughout his second year at Washington in 2003-04. He felt comfortable around his family and living at home was affordable. "I couldn't get him to move out," Tony Roy said. He rode back and forth in a gray 1996 Ford Taurus his father bought him while he was a Garfield senior.

The Taurus, like Roy, was a survivor. A tree split and a huge piece landed on the car, breaking the windshield and scratching the roof, while he was visiting Tiana Bardwell's Beacon Hill home. It was a hot day and he innocently parked the Taurus under the tree to take advantage of the shade. Roy and Allen together lifted the hefty tree debris off the vehicle while Bardwell backed the car out of the mess. In another incident, a basketball hoop fell on his vehicle, too, causing more damage. His parents kiddingly referred to the color of the Taurus as platinum. They were just trying to give this mundane and well-worn ride a more attractive image than it possessed.

"We all had busted cars in college," Robinson said. "We had no money. B-Roy had his Taurus and I had a 1992 Jeep Grand Cherokee, and the transmission didn't work. He had to take me home from the Romar camp once because it wouldn't run. The rear-view mirror always fell off his car because he played the music so loud, and he never used the mirror."

"He didn't like to drive," Gina Roy said. "He'd bring the car over to the house, so we would have two cars on his road trips and I could use it. I'd get in to take him back and he'd already be over in the passenger seat."

Unlike Roy, the Taurus only made it through three years of college. The car broke down and quit on him while he was driving on Interstate 90 to Bellevue when he was a junior. He coasted onto, and off, an exit ramp, and called his father to come rescue him. The repair bill estimate was more than the car was worth. The Taurus and Roy parted ways.

"I was a little down about it," he said. "I had told my dad that even if I went to the NBA I was going to keep that car."

It didn't look like anyone was headed to the NBA early in Roy's sophomore season at Washington. Instead of turning into the Fab Five, the Huskies went 0-5 to open the following Pac-10 season and were 5-8 overall. It was disastrous. It wasn't what anyone expected at all. Washington hadn't dropped its first five conference games in ten years, since Bender's first team had stumbled to a school-worst 5-22 record. Romar's second club looked totally lost. Fans called for the coach's head in a flurry of emails, letters, and phone calls to the Seattle newspapers. Players appeared numb as they emerged from the visitors' dressing room at the University of Oregon to explain the fifth consecutive defeat, an 84-74 decision.

Roy similarly suffered through his worst stretch of games at Washington. In four of five outings prior to the Oregon trip, he scored seven or fewer points. In three of those games, he collectively shot three for fifteen from the floor. It was a Pac-10 initiation, a lack of production, he had avoided until then.

Confidence was lagging for most Washington players. During that sluggish conference start, they lost to an unbeaten and fifth-ranked Stanford team in Palo Alto, 85-72, and the difference was palpable. While the Huskies showered, quietly packed their bags, and left the arena, Cardinal players celebrated in an animated locker room that was filled with inspirational quotations painted across the walls. Over their urinals, a Michael Jordan quote read as follows: "When we step on the floor, we're ready to play. If you're going to compete, we're going to dominate you." In the main dressing area, there was an Aristotle proverb for the Stanford players to consider: "We are what we repeatedly do. Excellence is not an act, but a habit."

Washington players didn't have that mind-set, at least not yet. "There are a couple of guys on that team who don't have the right attitude," Cardinal senior center Rob Little pointed out, adding that a couple of Romar's players wouldn't even shake his hand in the postgame receiving line.

Two games, one immediate and one at the end of the regular season, changed everything. After tanking at Oregon, the Huskies moved to Oregon State University and ended the misery in dramatic fashion. They erased a sixteen-point deficit over the final 6:10 of regulation play, with Roy feeding Robinson for a last-second three-pointer that forced overtime, and won 103-99. They returned to Seattle a new team.

In the turnaround that began in Corvallis, Oregon, the reenergized Huskies won five games in a row, eight of nine, and finally fourteen of sixteen to qualify for the NCAA Tournament—Washington's first postseason trip in five years. They beat Arizona three times in as many games. The first victory over the Wildcats came at home, 96-83, in a contest punctuated by a resounding Robinson backdoor dunk, with the aftermath of the play captured in a *Seattle Post-Intelligencer* photo that caught him hovering like a UFO well after the shot, his head almost even with the rim—an unforgettable image that was reprinted in *Sports Illustrated* and on T-shirts. "That Arizona dunk was my favorite dunk," Roy said. "I knew the play was coming. I'd seen it before. Still, I was stunned."

Roy threw one down on occasion, but he was more the steadying influence. After Washington picked up a second victory over the Wildcats in Tucson, Roy was named Pac-10 Player of the Week for the first time. He scored only twelve points in an 89-84 decision, fourth on his team in points that night, but demonstrated his versatility with eight assists and was rightfully rewarded. The once-forlorn Huskies kept moving in a positive direction.

"I haven't been around many turnarounds," Roy said. "Garfield was always winning. This is the greatest feeling of my life. I've never felt anything like this."

Beating Arizona and coach Lute Olson over and over validated Roy's decision to stay home. He never once questioned it. He figured it was up to him to reach the NBA, no one else. In his mind, whether he went through Seattle or Tucson to get there, it had no bearing on his future.

"Some guys don't have enough confidence in their game." Roy said. "I've never relied on a coach or point guard to make me a better player. I trust myself. I definitely thought about Arizona with Richard Jefferson, Gilbert Arenas, and all those guys in the pros. Meeting Lute Olson, I almost felt obliged to go there. But I figured if I played the same way at Washington as I would have at Arizona, I'd be a pro some day."

The Oregon State game turned around a season. The Stanford game signaled the Huskies, with their infusion of young talent, were for real. On the last day of the regular season, Roy and his teammates ruined a perfect season for the 26-0 and No. 1-ranked Cardinal, handing them a 75-62 setback before a sellout crowd at Edmundson Pavilion and an ABC national audience. Roy, who finished with twelve points and seven rebounds, and his teammates were swallowed up by a rush of emotional students stampeding the floor and celebrating a landmark moment.

The magical season came to an end in the first round of the NCAA Tournament in Columbus, Ohio. The Huskies lost a 102-100 footrace with a nonstop pressing and fast-breaking University of Alabama-Birmingham team, narrowing the gap at the end to make things close in a game they were never able to control. Roy played his typical unselfish game, contributing seven points, nine rebounds, and seven assists, but should have been used more. Still, Washington players left the Midwest more encouraged about their future than distraught over a tough postseason defeat.

Robinson and Roy finished 1-2 as the Huskies' scoring leaders, averaging 13.2 and 12.9 points per game, respectively. Five Washington players averaged in double figures. Roy also led the Huskies in rebounding with 5.3 per game. Yet this was unquestionably Robinson's team. Fans at home and on the road wanted to see the little guy perform his springy, acrobatic dunks, and he accommodated them as much as possible. He slammed down so many memorable dunks people started ranking and naming them.

Robinson was the only Washington player named to the ten-person All-Pac-10 team, selected by the head coaches. Roy was the only Huskies player among ten honorable-mention recipients, but thought he deserved better. He wasn't jealous of his teammate's recognition, but his omission from the top group made the competitor in him kick in.

"I think I should have been on [the first team], but it wasn't really my goal," Roy said, while scanning a sheet of paper that listed the all-conference breakdown. "I still want to go to the NCAA Tournament. I'll take that instead of this."

"I would have liked to see both of them on there," Romar said.

Roy and Robinson made a lot of things happen in a short amount of time, reinvigorating the Washington program. These old friends and their Huskies teammates finished 19-12 and second in both the Pac-10 regular season race and conference tourney. They tasted the NCAA Tournament, the school's first trip since the middle of the Bob Bender coaching era. They rejoiced and suffered together with extreme highs and lows. The way the top two guys interacted made it work.

"I think they both had a mutual respect for each other," Romar said. "I think Brandon will tell you Nate was the most exciting player to watch and Nate will tell you Brandon was the best player. Brandon let Nate have his space."

After two seasons at Washington, Robinson surprised everyone, including Roy, by submitting his name for the NBA draft and threatening to leave. Roy had no advance warning this was going to happen. He learned about it only when a FOX Sports broadcaster called him on his cell phone for reaction while he was leaving Edmundson Pavilion after an offseason workout. In the end, it was just a test run. Robinson attended the predraft camp in Chicago, auditioned for a number of teams, and then reclaimed his college eligibility, dissatisfied with his projected draft status as a second-rounder.

With everyone back for another year, Washington planned to keep the momentum rolling while encouraging Roy to take more of a lead role. He averaged fewer than ten shots per game as a sophomore. He came up with a career-high thirty points that season at UCLA, one of three Huskies on this versatile team to reach or exceed that scoring total during the season (Conroy and Robinson were the others), and actually questioned whether he had been selfish in doing it. He needed to become more comfortable in the spotlight.

"I can't remember a time where I took a lot of shots," Roy said. "There were games I scored a lot of points in my senior year at Garfield, but I didn't take a lot of shots. I've played unselfish my whole life. It's not something you can turn on and off."

"If you put ego aside for the betterment of the team, Brandon was the poster child for that," Romar said.

For the first two games of the 2004-05 season Roy was able to let loose. He scored twenty-three points against Seattle Pacific University in the opener and twenty-five points against the University of Utah in the first round of the Great Alaska Shootout. This was the Brandon Roy people had wanted to see since he signed on to play for the Huskies and demonstrated all those ultra-smooth moves. Somebody just had to wind him up and let him go. He was this free-wheeling player for just eleven more minutes before catastrophe struck.

On the second night in Anchorage, Roy felt a sharp pain in his right knee when he landed awkwardly in a game against the University of

Oklahoma. He came off the floor with 5:49 remaining in the opening half and was checked out by the team trainer. He played another minute before halftime, felt clicking in his knee, couldn't shake the discomfort, and was done for the trip.

On the following Monday, after the Huskies had beaten the University of Alabama 79-76 and won the Shootout without him, tests showed that Roy had suffered a lateral meniscus tear in the knee, which was opposite the one damaged three years earlier at Garfield High. Arthroscopic surgery was scheduled for Tuesday at University of Washington Medical Center. Roy was told he would miss four to six weeks while recovering. A momentary pall hung over a team ranked fourteenth in the country and capable of doing great things.

Unlike most athletes in this situation, Roy, who was clutching a yellow sheet of paper detailing the prognosis and a white pamphlet explaining the injury, pushed aside his disappointment long enough to hold a news conference. He was unfailingly positive as he answered reporters' questions about his injured hinge and his impending absence. Typical Roy, he was grateful that these media types wanted to know about his welfare.

"That's something I got from my mom," he said. "I always see the positive in everything. I called my mom after I saw the doctor. She said, 'You'll be fine. I remember the last time you did this.' Even the coach was a little down. This was our big year and one of his best players was down for a month. I said, 'Coach, I did this before. The knee will be fine.' "

The injury changed a lot of things overnight. Tre Simmons, Roy's Garfield teammate and a highly capable player, replaced him in the starting lineup. With a productive season—and he had gotten off to a very promising start—Roy had considered the possibility of entering the NBA draft again and passing up his senior season with the Huskies, same as Robinson. Now all of that seemed unlikely. Roy didn't have basketball options this time. The NCAA took away a player's remaining college eligibility if he filed the draft paperwork a second time, whether he was drafted or not. It now appeared Roy needed all four college years to properly interest the pros.

Roy sat out five games, including a 99-87 loss at Gonzaga University, the UW's first setback of the season. His team could have used him. He didn't travel to Loyola Marymount University for the Huskies' 100-93 victory and share in a game in which three of his teammates scored twenty points or more: Robinson had twenty-eight, Simmons twenty-six, and Jones twenty-one. To his benefit, Roy missed a turbulent ride home that night as the Alaska Airlines flight carrying the team from Los Angeles dipped and pitched in the wind in a frightening manner on final approach to Seattle, leaving Conroy howling in fear in the back of the plane. A crowded elevator stuck between floors couldn't have been more unnerving.

While most people pegged Roy for a late December return, he was back in three weeks. North Carolina State University was coming to Seattle and he couldn't miss the nationally televised game. The year before, the Huskies lost to the Atlantic Coast Conference team on the road, 77-72. Washington players had pointed to the rematch at home.

Roy took part in practices leading up to the game, tried out the knee, and had no significant swelling. He even assumed the role of North Carolina State's All-America candidate Julius Hodge, walking through plays to prepare his teammates for the real thing. Romar still wasn't going to let him play without parental approval. Tony Roy and Lou Hobson, the player's dad and AAU coach, watched the final workout, were satisfied with Brandon's mobility, and gave him the go-ahead to return to action.

Yet right before the game, Roy's knee suddenly felt sore and he decided he wasn't going to play. Midway through the first half, the knee still felt tight and he wasn't going to play. Finally, Romar asked him if he wanted to go in. Roy took a quick side trip off the floor to ride a stationary bike, loosened up, and returned to log eighteen minutes. Adrenaline kicked in, and he was the difference in Washington's 68-64 victory. He scored ten points, all in the second half, most down the stretch, including a left-handed tip jam that brought people squealing out of their seats.

With Roy back on a limited basis, depending on his knee soreness, he and Romar cut a deal. Roy could play when he felt able, but he wouldn't start, to prevent team chemistry from being compromised, with him in and out of uniform from one game to the next. He sat out four of the next eight games for precautionary reasons before appearing in the final eighteen. He actually started once more as an emergency fill-in, at Oregon, when

Jones was too ill with the flu to go out for the opening tip. Roy also had his moments of brilliance.

Roy turned in consecutive double-double performances, picking up twenty points and thirteen rebounds in an 82-70 victory at home over UCLA, and eighteen points and ten rebounds in the game against the Ducks, a 95-88 overtime win in which he played a season-high thirty-eight minutes and fouled out. Late in the season, Stanford coach Trent Johnson felt compelled to describe Roy as "un-guardable," even with the Huskies swingman coming off the bench and not at full strength.

"We had an agreement that he would just come off the bench," Romar said. "It wouldn't be disruptive. I don't think that was his ideal choice. He never told me that. I don't think someone else could have handled it. Jon Brockman might have been the most unselfish player we've had here, but I don't think he could have handled it. Brandon dealt with it."

A late-season flop at Oregon State, with Roy back in a reserve role and the Huskies taking a 90-73 pounding, brought up the outside suggestion from fans and media that maybe he should be starting again after all. Instead, Washington players held an hour-long team meeting, with some of them standing up and apologizing to the others for their tepid performances. Otherwise, things remained status quo.

"There is no pressure on me to be in the lineup," Roy said, shrugging off the idea. "I'm going to play just as hard coming off the bench or starting. I'm kind of in a groove coming off the bench."

Who could argue? The Huskies finished second in the conference race to UCLA again, but won the Pac-10 tourney for the first time, upsetting Arizona 81-72 in the championship game at the Staples Center in Los Angeles. On selection Sunday, they received an unexpected reward and ultimate respect—the Huskies were singled out as one of the four No. 1 seeds in the NCAA Tournament, joining the University of Illinois, University of North Carolina, and Duke University. Roy sat with his teammates at Edmundson Pavilion, surrounded by fans, and watched the bracket announcement on CBS. While he had no insider knowledge about what was revealed on the big screen in front of him, he must have had a cosmic connection to his long-term basketball prospects that Sunday afternoon—he showed up wearing a Portland Trail Blazers cap.

The most successful Washington team in modern times finished 29-6, tying the school record for most victories in a season. The Huskies made it to the Sweet Sixteen round, easily beating the University of Montana 88-77 and University of Pacific 97-79 in Boise, Idaho, before they were eliminated by the University of Louisville 93-79 in a physical game in Albuquerque, New Mexico. Against the Cardinals, the Roy-Robinson tandem came to an end after a glorious three-year run with the Huskies. They had shared in consecutive NCAA Tournament appearances. They had played off each other better than any two collegiate players bound for NBA careers could hope. Robinson grabbed most of the headlines when they were together, but he was the last one to undervalue Roy's ability.

"We had a good time playing together," Robinson said. "It was fun. It's weird when people looked at him, because they really don't know who Brandon was. I've been watching him since fifth grade, and I believed in him so much."

Roy seemed to wear down at the end. His knee had been through a lot. He had a decent junior season statistically, averaging 12.8 points and five rebounds per game, nearly matching his numbers from the year before when he was fully healthy. It still wasn't nearly what those close to the program envisioned from him.

Roy now had to determine his future, though his injury seemed to limit his options. Would he exit with fellow starters Robinson, Conroy, and Simmons, and turn to the NBA? Or would he share himself with a bunch of incoming freshmen and others and try to improve his draft status, which was no better than a second-rounder before and after incurring the knee injury? While the answer seemed obvious, college basketball players in general had a history of making irrational decisions when it came to pro basketball, leaving some doubt.

On April 25, 2005, with interested teammates Jamaal Williams and Bobby Jones looking on, Roy held a news conference to announce he was returning to Washington to play as a senior. This was somewhat ironic, considering he once tried to skip the college ranks and go directly to the pros out of Garfield High School.

"I was surprised because we had a great year and been a No. 1 seed," Jones said. "After the tournament, I was thinking that next season was going to be tough because everybody was leaving. Usually ninety percent of the players in that situation will leave. Why wouldn't you go?"

Roy talked about his knee, his loyalty to the program, and the strong likelihood that Martell Webster, a Seattle high school kid and Huskies recruit, was headed to the pros. Webster, in fact, would beat Roy to Portland by a full year, selected by the Trail Blazers with the sixth pick overall in the 2005 draft, the same draft slot Roy would occupy twelve months later.

As Roy sat in front of a room filled with reporters, coaches, and those teammates, he seemed relieved that his basketball future was decided. He was anxious to play in the NBA, but he needed to go about it the right way. Extreme patience, something he had demonstrated on the basketball floor, now seemed invaluable to him away from the court. This was a money decision, a chance for Roy to show the pros what he was made of without a test score hanging over him, without Robinson overshadowing him or without a weakened knee slowing him, and it all made sense.

"I didn't want to go through the back door," Roy said. "I wanted to go through the front door."

Of course, if there was a crowded elevator involved in reaching the NBA's ground floor, he would have taken the stairs to get there.

CHAPTER 10

MAKING OF A LOTTERY PICK

B randon Roy had solid credentials that were soon spectacular. In 2006, he was voted the best basketball player in the Pac-10 Conference by its coaches, and was perhaps the best college player in the country. On a Friday night in Washington, D.C., a purple-clad Roy was easily the best player on the floor in the NCAA Tournament against a mighty University of Connecticut team full of future NBA players.

This was a sort of March Madness people elsewhere around the country hadn't counted on. Roy practically did whatever he wanted. He hit from three-point range under heavy guard. He threw a no-look pass to an open University of Washington teammate for an easy score. He stripped the ball off the dribble from UConn reserve guard Craig Austrie, embarrassing his opponent as he raced in and dunked with two hands.

The veteran CBS broadcasting crew of Verne Lundquist and Bill Raferty couldn't praise Roy enough. They treated him as if he were some new discovery, which he was to people tuning into the broadcast. The Big East team couldn't stop Roy with traditional means. It managed to find another way.

With his Washington team comfortably on top 53-45 in a matchup of teams that both answered to the nickname Huskies, Roy was fourteen minutes from advancing to the NCAA Tournament's Elite Eight against a beatable George Mason team when everything came undone at the Verizon Center. It wasn't planned. It just happened. The overly physical nature of the game brought out a brief yet damaging display of temper at the worst possible moment.

Attempting to hang close to Rudy Gay on defense, Roy was trailing him when he drew contact from UConn's six-foot-eleven forward Josh Boone, who leaned over and slammed into him with a forceful shoulder while setting a screen alongside the foul lane. A whistle sounded. Everybody stopped except Gay, who struck Roy in the stomach with a sharp and unnecessary elbow at the foul line, well after everyone else had stopped playing. Two hard shots to the body in the same play sequence, especially the last one, were more than Roy could bear. He went nose to nose with Gay. Angry words were exchanged. Officials quickly separated them, with one of the referees emphatically gesturing for Roy to head to his bench as if it were a boxing corner. A double technical foul was assessed, penalizing both teams. Nothing too outlandish or damaging had taken place, or so it seemed.

Everything would have been fine for Seattle's Huskies and their game-breaking player to that point, except that one of referees also called a separate foul on Roy. Television replays showed Boone moving into the Washington player with a solid body shot, hardly the stationary pick that was permitted by the rulebook, but it didn't matter. Now saddled with four personal fouls (counting the technical), Roy sat for the next seven minutes, momentum was lost, and eventually so was this overly competitive contest, 98-92 in overtime. Roy fouled out with eleven seconds remaining in the extra session, trying to retrieve the ball following an errant pass thrown by panicked teammate Joel Smith.

Afterward, in a spacious interview room full of newspaper and TV reporters on tight deadlines, the controversial, game-changing play midway through the second half was brought up for discussion and dissected. In detail, it was viewed somewhat differently by the players involved. In the end, there was general agreement by both that it was an unfortunate byproduct of a spirited game with a lot riding on it. Gay and Roy already had settled their differences in the traditional postgame receiving line before sitting down separately in front of the assembled press corps.

"I made an aggressive move and I bumped him," said Gay, choosing a verb that seemed to greatly water down the elbow later shown over and over on replays. "It was all in the heat of the battle. It wasn't intentional, but he didn't know that. I talked to him after the game and said I'd see him again. He's a good guy."

Roy's explanation was a little more pointed, though he seemed too exhausted to get further worked up about it. "He elbowed me in the stomach and it was a cheap shot," Roy said more descriptively. "I said, 'Watch that!' He said, 'Get that shit out of my face!' The other guy is exploding and I didn't do anything, but it looked bad."

There were many plays that impacted the outcome of the game. Washington senior center Mike Jensen's ill-conceived foul in the closing moments of regulation play was glaring, but he repeatedly had been out of position on the defensive end all game. A tying three-pointer from Connecticut's Rashad Anderson from twenty-five feet with 2.2 seconds left in regulation play was heroic. Smith's overtime pass, after he became rattled under pressure and threw it away, figured strongly in the outcome. However, Roy's reaction, with a rare display of anger, was not only counter to his usual cool demeanor but a Cinderella deal-breaker.

"If he hadn't got that technical, we probably go on and win that game," Washington coach Lorenzo Romar acknowledged, his team having led by as many as eleven points. "They were on the verge of cracking."

"The situation with Rudy wasn't even that bad," former Huskies teammate Bobby Jones said. "If that hadn't happened, we definitely would have been in the Final Four."

It was the only real blot on a superlative senior season for Roy, a player fully capable of leading an unsung team to the Final Four. While the outcome was hugely disappointing, a rare opportunity lost, in no way did it diminish the high-level performance turned in by the Huskies' showcase player over five entertaining months. At Washington, only six-foot-seven center Bob Houbregs had received more individual accolades and actually delivered his team to the NCAA's promised land—a 1953 Final Four berth in a far more navigable twenty-two team tournament bracket.

Coincidentally, Houbregs, a prolific 25.6-point scorer named the college game's 1952-53 player of the year, was removed from his third postseason game that year, a semifinals matchup against the University of Kansas in Kansas City, in a controversial manner maddeningly similar to Roy's. Jayhawks players, under their coach's orders, repeatedly had jumped into the Washington big man's path as he crossed the midcourt line, drawing phantom offensive fouls. They effectively disqualified Houbregs with his fifth personal foul early in the second half and eliminated his team, which some had pegged as the tourney favorite, from title contention.

Houbregs, who later was an NBA player, Seattle SuperSonics general manager, and Converse executive, had stayed close to the Washington basketball program, strongly endorsing Romar's coaching efforts. A season-ticket holder, Houbregs made the one hundred and twenty-mile round-trip on Interstate 5 from his Olympia home to attend as many games at Edmundson Pavilion as he could, especially when Roy played. He sat in an aisle seat to accommodate his long, arthritic legs, at the same end of the gym in which his retired jersey No. 25 hung overhead, the only digit in school history pulled from service to that point. He was a devoted fan of Brandon Roy.

Houbregs considered this unique player a throwback to his simpler college basketball times, while recognizing Roy came equipped with all of the flashier, modern-day nuances. Most players didn't share the ball like Roy did. In Houbregs's day, everyone did. "I wish they would go through him every play," he said. "He passes so well."

Roy's basketball plans initially never included his senior year at Washington. He tried to go directly to the NBA out of high school. His redrawn strategy had him playing no more than three college seasons for the Huskies. Yet things changed for him when he least expected it. He injured his right knee and missed a third of his junior season. He agreed to come off the bench as a reserve player that year while recovering from in-season arthroscopic surgery and regaining his form. He wasn't able to properly showcase his special skills for a Pac-10 Tournament champion and the school's first No. 1-seeded NCAA qualifier, a team that was filled with pro basketball prospects.

"How was this guy going to go to the league when he doesn't even start for his team?" was a question posed by University of Arizona center

Channing Frye, who briefly was a Portland Trail Blazers teammate of Roy's. "We just saw a role player in Brandon."

In Seattle, Roy's longtime Garfield and college teammates, Will Conroy and Tre Simmons, had used up their college eligibility, while his childhood friend Nate Robinson had settled on NBA early entry after delaying it once. Touted incoming recruit Martell Webster from nearby Seattle Preparatory School wasn't going to bypass the pros to spend a season at Washington, and everyone knew it. Another desired recruit, Kentwood High School guard Rodney Stuckey, also a future pro, had listed the Huskies as his first college choice, but couldn't qualify academically and had to leave the Seattle area and enroll across the state at Eastern Washington. A logical step was for Roy to move on, too. Yet with the nonstop program turnover, combined with his sore knee, plus a feeling of unfinished business and a sense of loyalty to the program, Roy stayed put.

"I loved playing with Nate and Will, but to stand on my own two feet with this team would make me a better player and more focused," Roy said of the decision. "All three of us leaving would have put the team in a bind. I felt I could be that glue. I could be one of the most successful guys at the University of Washington. Think of U-Dub history and you would bring up Brandon Roy."

Two things had to happen for him to achieve Seattle basketball immortality. His right knee needed to be sound again. With all the medical advances in place in the sporting world for treating this type of injury, there was no reason to think that wouldn't happen. Much more of a struggle would be persuading Roy to become the focus of attention. He would be asked by his Huskies coaches to be a lot greedier with a basketball in his hands, rather than outwardly concerned about everyone else's touches.

Pickup-game players throughout Seattle, guys with barely an ounce of the talent that Roy possessed, were amazed when they teamed with him during the summer at the University of Washington or any number of gyms throughout the city and he regularly fed them the basketball, something that didn't usually happen when this sort of mismatch of talent ran the floor together. Roy was now being asked by Romar to make a change in his lifelong behavior, stretching back to his childhood, to move into unfamiliar territory. Admittedly, it was an adjustment for him.

"Just by nature, I'm one of those guys who defers," Roy said. "Growing up with my brother and sister, if we all wanted something, I'd say, 'I don't need it. I can go without it.' With Nate, Will, and Tre, at times I was almost a pushover. It was easier for Brandon to deal with it instead of Nate or Will or Tre. I just wanted to win and do whatever I could to make that happen, because I had told so many people it was going to be good at the University of Washington. I had to defer. Somebody had to make us a team."

Romar's goal now was to make this Brandon Roy's team, to make him the main attraction. This was not as easy as it sounded. There were still veteran players on board—for instance, fellow seniors Jamaal Williams and Jones, who could score in bunches and were reliable teammates. There were highly regarded freshmen coming in, Jon Brockman and Justin Dentmon to name two, who were quite capable of putting the ball in the basket and getting the job done as instant Huskies starters.

Yet to make everything work in the best possible manner and take total advantage of a special skill set, this had to be Roy's big stage. He still needed some prodding to climb onto it. He was forced to run wind sprints in early fall practices by his coaches for not being assertive enough, when normally that was a penalty for being way too single-minded. Being the focus guy for the Huskies wasn't a totally new concept for Roy, but it had to develop.

"Even though Brandon was not the leading scorer last season, when we needed a basket we went to Brandon," Romar pointed out, demonstrating Roy's importance. "Nate made hustle plays and provided energy. With Tre, we went to him when we got going. But late in games, when we had a problem scoring, we went to Brandon."

The 2005-06 season began and not much was different at all about Roy's game. In the Huskies' first ten games, all victories, he led the team in scoring just three times and averaged only nine shots per game. He was still the provider, just not the scoring machine as promised. In a 99-95 home victory over Gonzaga University, a scoring slugfest that featured Bulldogs junior forward Adam Morrison serving up a career-tying 43 points in defeat,

Roy scored just 10 points. He was fifth in scoring in the Huskies' side of the box score that night, trailing Williams's 22, Dentmon's 17, Jones's 15, and Ryan Appleby's 14. Roy was supposed to be doing what Morrison had done, only in this case he seemed to be more careful than ever not to step on anyone's toes, moving in the opposite direction of stardom. But his team still won.

Roy wasn't lacking any respect from Gonzaga and its lottery-pick candidate, though. During a second-half lull, the six-foot-eight Morrison sidled up to him on the foul line and casually remarked, "Hey, Roy, I'm going to see you in June." The reference was to the upcoming NBA draft. Roy was so startled by the comment that all he could do was laugh out loud. Morrison kept talking, telling Roy he respected his game. In turn, Roy repaid the compliment with one of his own, informing Morrison that he was a fan of his, too. At a moment like this, with the outcome in question and everyone else oblivious to the players' floor-level dialogue, there had to be a good comeback to punctuate this impromptu meeting. In serious foul trouble at the time and feeling as if he were a victim of Morrison's undetected tugs and clever pushes, Roy couldn't resist and provided an appropriate punch line. "In June, there won't be any refs," he wisecracked.

To the national and local media, Romar had gone out of his way to promote the wondrous skills of a new-look Roy, to predict untold greatness for him, to lobby for coast-to-coast attention for him. Throughout November and December, people wanted to know what had happened to this special player the Huskies coach had so richly described, because that player hadn't shown up. "In the preseason, people kept asking me, 'Where's this All-American you keep talking about?' " Romar said.

Roy usually preferred a low profile, both on and off the basketball court. It was his nature. Unlike most college students, who felt the need to prowl the Washington campus or the city, who went searching for weekend parties or other forms of entertainment, or who simply wanted to get out and see or be seen, Roy was an incurable homebody. Teammates tried their best to include him in their social outings. There were only occasional Roy sightings in some late-night college setting.

"He kept it as simple as possible," Jones said. "We were going to bars and frat parties and I'd invite him, but he wouldn't do it. He'd stay home. Every so often he'd come out and we'd make a big deal about it. He kind of had an old-man mentality."

"I never thought about doing anything except how was I going to get to practice the next day," Roy said of the partying scene he eschewed. "Some guys, football players, I had to ask, 'How can you do that?' Some guys could do it. I had to recover. I had to get my rest. I couldn't do any of that."

It took a while, but Roy finally let loose in a big way when the Pac-10 schedule opened. With the Huskies hosting the Arizona schools at home, his coming-out party was unforgettable. Roy scored a career-best thirty-five points against outmanned Arizona State University in a 91-67 victory. "All I know was he was hands down the best basketball player I'd seen," said Jeff Pendergraph, then a Sun Devils freshman center and later a Portland Trail Blazers teammate. "I'd never seen anyone score like him."

Two days later, Roy dropped another thirty-five points on a tougher University of Arizona team. Against the Wildcats, he twice brought the crowd out of its seats by hitting extra-long, heavily guarded three-pointers right before the regulation and overtime buzzers sounded, prolonging a game the Huskies would ultimately lose 96-95. Even though the outcome wasn't the preferred one, Roy had finally taken over a college game on command, and there was no turning back.

In those two outings, Roy had let fly with twenty-two and twenty-nine shots, the two highest numbers of field-goal attempts in his college career, and made a combined twenty-six shots in the series. He had to be thinking this center-of-attention stuff wasn't so bad after all.

"At the beginning of the season, he was playing okay, but he wasn't playing the way people thought he should be playing," Appleby pointed out. "Arizona was big confidence-builder for him. It seemed like whenever a shot or pass had to be made, he made it. He was hitting thirty-five-foot threes. He played such a perfect game that day."

A much more relaxed Roy said at the time: "I dealt with heavy pressure. The good thing was, I dealt with it early in the season."

It was game on for Roy. He led the Huskies in scoring in eighteen of the team's final twenty-three games, a streak that included nine consecutive contests through the heart of the Pac-10 race. Two weeks after his break-out home stand, Roy came up with a twenty-three-point, twelve-rebound showing in an 87-77 victory over USC in Los Angeles, leading then-Trojans coach Tim Floyd to remark, "I'll be glad when he graduates." Two nights later at Pauley Pavilion, Roy's favorite opposing Pac-10 gym, UCLA focused most of its defensive attention on him, limiting the guard to ten points on just nine shots. However, Roy stayed calm and patient enough to direct his team to a huge 69-65 upset of the Bruins, just the third victory for Washington in forty-one tries in that hallowed arena overflowing with national championship banners and winning tradition. "I'll be disappointed if we don't go deep in the tournament," Roy said afterward, already looking ahead to the NCAAs.

Roy took over this team in other ways, too. Two weeks later, the Huskies blew a game at Stanford University in an incredibly reckless manner. Dentmon, a freshman, bumped the Cardinal's Chris Hernandez on a prayer of a three-point shot attempt at the buzzer, sending Hernandez to the foul line. Hernandez, a poised and unflappable senior, sank three free throws without much trouble that forced overtime and led to a 75-67 defeat for Washington.

Young Dentmon was so despondent over the play he initially declined to speak to three Seattle beat reporters who had entered the Huskies locker room in search of postgame quotes, particularly his. Overprotective team trainer Brett Brungardt attempted to shield Dentmon from the media, forcefully warning them to stay away from the freshman guard. Dentmon was now seated in front of his locker, still in uniform, and trying to hide with nowhere to go.

A white towel wrapped around him, Roy calmly walked over, interceded, and whispered a few words into the first-year player's ear. Dentmon agreed to make himself available for media questioning in the hallway a few minutes later, a session that would turn out painless for everyone involved. Roy simply reminded his teammate about his team responsibilities, win or lose, a true veteran move on his part. There were subsequent pep talks, too.

"We told him, 'You're our point guard and we need you for the rest of the season, and you have to come back with a nice attitude and we need you to get better. We win games as a team and we lose games as a team. We just have to keep fighting. We can't give up hope,' " Roy said. "I don't think he was sure how we were going to respond to him. He was a little down. He was pretty upset he made that mistake."

Roy also was privy to media needs and the benefits of receiving good press. Always accessible, whether happy or sad, injured or healthy, the Washington guard candidly explained his longstanding approach with reporters before his senior season began.

"I love talking to the media," he said. "I'm not a guy who tries to duck the media. It's right for the fans to hear what we have to say. If the media just said stuff and we didn't voice our opinions, we'd be upset about that. I try to make myself available."

The Huskies finished second to UCLA in the conference race that season for the second year in a row, but they swept the Bruins in their 2005-06 season series. This was big. It was just the third time this had happened in school history, matching Washington's 1950-51 and 1986-87 teams. Roy had twenty points and seven assists in the 70-67 clincher over UCLA in Seattle, and was still feeling competitive afterward. "We have to make sure the good Husky basketball team shows up every night," he said. "I think more than anybody, UCLA hates it when we beat them. It's really bothering them that we have their number now."

Traveling to Oregon a week later, Roy had a legitimate shot at picking up his first career triple-double performance against Oregon State University, but the contest got out of hand and he was pulled early in the second half of a 96-63 victory. He finished with twenty-five points, eight rebounds, and nine assists. With two minutes remaining, Romar walked by Roy on the bench and told him that he was sorry that the personal milestone had eluded him but there was really nothing he could do about it, outside of dishonoring a badly beaten opponent by putting Roy back in. Roy shrugged it off, hardly concerned about stats. If nothing else, he had put on an impressive showing for his parents, guiding the Huskies to a sweep of the Oregon schools while they traveled with the team for the first time.

By now, it was obvious to everyone on the West Coast what kind of season Roy was having. Offering up a twenty-seven-point effort that included several clutch shots, he led the Huskies to a 73-62 victory at home over third-place University of California, drawing the following postgame assessment from Golden Bears coach Ben Braun: "I thought he had a huge year. I thought he took his team over the hump. I thought Brandon Roy took his team and put it on his back, and he was phenomenal."

Accompanied by his parents, a beaming Roy walked out before the California game and was honored as part of Washington's Senior Day celebration, something he and a lot of other people probably had thought was not possible, for many reasons, with the NBA always beckoning and those test scores keeping him sidelined.

On the following Monday, the consistently good Roy was selected as Pac-10 Player of the Week for the third consecutive week, joining former Arizona State guard Eddie House as the only players in conference history to pull off this feat. Opponents throughout the Pac-10 needed no convincing about Roy's talent level.

"He always had something I liked about his game," said Washington State University guard Kyle Weaver, later an NBA player for the Oklahoma City Thunder. "He played like no other. He was the one guy I always liked, and I thought once he got to the NBA he would do more than he did in college."

To close out the regular season schedule, the Huskies played at Arizona, possibly the toughest place in the Pac-10 to win a road game. Each time Roy touched the ball, the students derisively chanted, "SATs, SATs, SATs," unwilling to let him forget a far more difficult time in his college experience. Of course, they would have preferred to have him in a Wildcats uniform, cheering his every move instead. With sixteen points and eleven rebounds, he helped avenge the overtime loss to Arizona in Seattle, by leading his team to a 70-67 victory. Roy wasn't quite a finished product just yet, but he was close. He still had an unselfish streak that was hard to shake.

With more than thirteen minutes remaining and the Wildcats up by twelve points, Washington assistant coach Cameron Dollar had to remind Roy once more it was time to exert his will on the basketball court. The guard did as he was instructed, scoring ten points and doling out three assists down the stretch, and a masterful upset in Tucson was complete.

Lute Olson could only reflect on what might have been had he successfully persuaded the Garfield kid four years earlier to come to Tucson and play. Olson probably wouldn't have experienced too many losses, if any, at home during that time.

"When I watched him play in high school, it was a case of when he wanted to do it he could completely dominate," Olson said of the graceful player. "He didn't play as intense as he does now. Lorenzo has got him playing really hard. There was never any question about his ability. I think this would have been a good situation here for him, too. He needed to be in an up-tempo style. He'd be good in any style of play, but he's really good in an up-tempo style. He makes more good decisions with the ball. He's going to be an outstanding pro."

As the postseason approached, the various All-America teams were released. Not everyone did their homework in determining individual honors. The U. S. Basketball Writers Association (USBWA) unveiled its ten finalists for the Oscar Robertson Award, given to the nation's top college player, and Roy was not on this list. In the end, however, Roy mysteriously was included as one of five players selected on the USBWA's All-America first team.

What happened was this: the USBWA received such a negative reaction for omitting Roy, particularly from CBSSports.com's vitriolic columnist Gregg Doyel, that it privately reversed itself. The national media organization, headed by ESPN college basketball analyst Andy Katz, rightfully deserved to be bashed for omitting Roy in the first place, but at least deserved credit for taking measures to right a wrong.

"We did look kind of ridiculous," said John Akers, *Basketball Times* editor and one of the dozen or so USBWA voters. "It was a glaring omission. Later I remember writing in retrospect that Brandon should have been the player of the year. Both [co-MVPs] J.J. Redick and Adam Morrison had bad Marches."

Nationwide respect still remained a widespread issue for the Huskies guard, prompting Romar to do some late-season campaigning. The coach came to his weekly news conference armed with compelling information, noting Roy's presence among the leaders in nine of thirteen Pac-10 statistical categories, an amazing display of basketball versatility. Most Internet sites that offered mock NBA drafts still had Roy as a middle first-round pick, usually listed fifteen to eighteen, but hovering pro scouts and sports agents now had a much higher opinion of him.

"I don't know of any player in America doing as many things as he is to help his basketball team," Romar pointed out without any prodding.

Four tournament games went a long way toward solidifying Roy's basketball reputation as an elite player. He scored thirty points against the University of Oregon in a Pac-10 Tournament loss, and twenty-eight, twenty-one, and twenty points in the NCAA Tournament against Utah State University, the University of Illinois, and Connecticut, respectively. He forced opponents to continually change defenders against him. He repeatedly made opponents look silly.

On March 16, 2006, first-round games at San Diego State's Cox Arena were delayed more than an hour while authorities evacuated the area, brought in explosives-sniffing dogs, and checked out a potential bomb scare. A suspicious package that turned out to be harmless was found on a condiment cart. The delay did nothing to slow Roy in his opening game against Utah State. Following a 75-61 defeat to Washington that was engineered by the senior guard, Utah State coach Stew Morrill readily conceded: "We really had no answer for him."

Roy's cover was effectively blown against Illinois, before he played the high-powered Big Ten team. During a news conference for the second-round NCAA matchup, Illini senior point-guard Dee Brown sat at a front table and admitted to being a full-fledged hoops junkie, regularly staying up well past midnight during the week to get his fix of cable television college basketball games. Roy was no stranger to him at all. Brown actually scoffed when asked what he knew about the cornerstone of the Huskies' team.

"I could see right away he was a player, and he could do so many things," Brown said. "You don't need to tell me how good Brandon Roy is."

Brown was even more of a believer the next day after Roy directed the Huskies to a hard-pressed 67-64 victory, eliminating his Illini. Now everyone wanted to know more about this gifted Washington player. Following his twenty-one-point, seven-rebound, and three-assist showing, Roy stood in a narrow hallway in a sweaty uniform for the longest time at Cox Arena, fielding questions from representatives of several national media outlets, this following his required visit to the NCAA's postgame interview area. With the next game in progress just around the corner, reporters asked Roy about that shipping-container job, his SAT struggles, and his early flirtation with the NBA. *Sports Illustrated's* Phil Taylor was among the most inquisitive in the group, later producing a story in the national magazine entitled "Coming Out Party," suggesting Roy was an unknown outside of the Pac-10 until this postseason performance against Illinois.

Roy continued to impress people with his athletic ability, even his teammates. Before facing Connecticut in the Sweet Sixteen round, Romar led his team through a spirited workout at George Washington University in the nation's capital. Everybody was in a good mood. For whatever reason, the players got into a debate about who was the fastest on this Huskies team. Bobby Jones was a logical choice. Joel Smith was the other leading candidate. To keep the mood light, Romar put the players to the test and had them race each other. Roy easily won the competition.

"Nobody picked me," Roy said. "Everybody said Bobby or Joel. I thought I could beat those guys."

"He's quicker than people think," Romar said.

Although his NCAA Tournament ended with a shoulder blow followed by a sharp forearm to the gut, Roy's decision to use all of his college eligibility was the right one, and not the least bit painful otherwise. He became a first-team Associated Press (AP) All-American, just the third for the Washington basketball program, joining 1934 point guard Hal Lee and Houbregs. Roy shared top AP honors with Duke's J. J. Redick and Shelden Williams, Villanova University's Randy Foye, and Gonzaga's Adam Morrison. Roy averaged 20.2 points, 5.6 rebounds, and 4.1 assists as a senior, becoming just the tenth different Huskies player in program history to average twenty points per game in a season.

Roy had elevated himself to lottery-pick status and stood to make a lot more money by having delayed his NBA career. He developed better stamina. His jump shot was vastly improved. His confidence was at an all-time high. He learned how to take charge on the floor, yet not see his game veer off selfishly in the process. He became the total package as a basketball player, something that might not have happened quite so readily had he departed the college scene early.

Roy left school two quarters shy of obtaining a bachelor's degree in American ethnic studies, carrying a 2.5 grade-point average. After letting high school slide in a big way and enduring all those earlier SAT struggles, he had become an average college student, which was a significant upgrade. He had tutorial help whenever he needed it at Washington. He satisfied his foreign language requirement with a Swahili class that he enjoyed. He also promised his parents he would return and obtain his diploma.

"He discovered it wasn't his ambition to get straight As, but he went to class and was responsible, and he did what he needed to do," Romar said.

Roy took an unconventional route to pro basketball for someone so talented, and he was about to be rewarded for it. He harkened back to the day he attempted NBA early entry and sort of shook his head. Everything had worked out for the best.

"Honestly, I didn't think I was going to be here as a senior," Roy admitted as he awaited the 2006 NBA draft. "I didn't understand how fun college basketball was. I almost wish I had another year."

CHAPTER 11

NBA AUDITIONS

Throughout his senior season at Washington, Brandon Roy was shielded from direct contact from sports agents. All inquiries and proposals were directed to his Huskies coach, Lorenzo Romar, and to his AAU coach, Lou Hobson, with no exceptions. That didn't stop those aggressive people from lining the lobby of the Huskies' Washington, D.C. hotel in an intrusive manner, hoping to be seen immediately after Roy and his teammates had suffered their gut-wrenching 98-92 loss in overtime to the University of Connecticut in the 2006 NCAA Tournament with the player's collegiate eligibility officially expired. However, agents found Roy extra challenging and hardly gullible in this pro basketball recruiting process.

"Every agent, crooked or straight, had to come at me straight," Roy said. "Players were asking me during the season, 'What are you getting?' and I said, 'I'm getting nothing.' Agents that were shady knew they had to straighten up to even get a sit-down with me."

"Brandon is really smart," said Jamal Crawford, his close friend from Seattle, a guard for the New York Knicks at the time and someone well versed on agents. "He watches people."

Roy settled on Arn Tellem's sports agency, which had merged into the Wasserman Media Group, specifically choosing Bob Myers to represent him. There was a connection that helped facilitate this business arrangement. Myers had been a reserve forward for UCLA's 1995 national championship team and someone who had played for Romar, then a Bruins assistant coach.

Myers wanted to handle all of Roy's personal needs. He was young and hardworking. He promised to make the Huskies guard his top priority, and Roy liked that. Romar gave Myers a favorable reference. Seattle attorney Rich Padden, Roy's unofficial advisor, sat in on a meeting with the agent and offered his blessing, too. More important, the money changing hands between the player and his handlers was fair. The agency would receive three percent of Roy's salary, and fifteen percent of endorsements from shoe, trading card, and other dealings.

Everything was about substance and maintaining a proper image for Roy, though the prospect of earning a guaranteed $7 million to $11 million just for playing basketball over the next couple of years was something that needed to be properly managed. Conservative by nature, he had to be talked into buying the new $70,000 Cadillac Escalade he had expressed interest in, $6,000 wheel rims and $2,000 top-of-the-line stereo included. Roy wanted to wait until his pro destination was determined, but he finally gave in at his father's urging and allowed himself this early reward. Otherwise, he was adamant about not letting money change him or spending it wildly.

"I not only have to deal with the pressure of being drafted, but I also have to deal with the pressure of being who I am," Roy said, explaining the challenging crossroad of acquiring wealth and maintaining humility. "What makes me who I am is being honest. That's who I am. It's nothing I have to change. At the same time, I don't want to throw it into anybody's face."

The Wasserman Group liked what it had seen and heard. It had to have this guy in its portfolio. Roy appeared to be an endorsement magnet, not to mention the perfect, low-maintenance NBA client. He was an agent's dream. He had advertisement potential written all over him. All he had to do was act and play naturally, and lots of people would want to associate with him.

"Plenty of great players don't get marketed and a lot of All-Stars don't get marketed," Myers said. "Tim Duncan is not that heavily marketed, because it's harder to market a big guy and he doesn't have great charisma, which is not a negative on him. People relate more to a Tracy McGrady or a Dwyane Wade. I think Brandon has that. He has the ability to be an All-Star and be a person kids want to emulate."

While others might have been plotting how many cars and houses they could purchase for themselves, Roy talked about buying his parents a home; paying the tuition at a performance arts school for his sister, something his parents couldn't readily afford; covering the remaining two years of college tuition for Cole Allen, as a gesture of their longtime friendship; and maybe finding a new car for his older brother, Ed. Brandon Roy wasn't going to let anyone sponge off him and his newfound riches, but made it clear he was very open to supporting positive pursuits of those closest to him.

"I almost feel like the fairy godmother," Roy said. "Instead of sitting around and having people live off me, I can put them in a position to be successful themselves. I'm a giver more than a receiver. I get an extra amount of pleasure in giving."

With the agent selection out of the way, Roy now had to sell his basketball skills. He conducted most NBA draft workouts in Los Angeles, because the Wasserman Media Group was based there. These sessions were often held at the Santa Monica High School gym or the home of Los Angeles Lakers super-fan Steve Jackson, whose private, indoor basketball court was built to resemble a mini-Staples Center. A serious memorabilia collector, Jackson had a piece of flooring from the old Los Angeles Forum, the Lakers' previous home court, mounted on the wall of his personal basketball shrine. It was signed by Magic Johnson, Kobe Bryant, and others, and now by Brandon Roy.

It was an overly hectic three months for Roy leading up to the draft. However, he found time to dream a little about what was coming next for him. Making a rare admission for a high lottery pick, Roy caught himself fantasizing about wearing the uniforms of the Trail Blazers and the Lakers. Los Angeles would have to trade up to get him, though. Portland had the fourth pick, but already had made it publicly known it was committed to acquiring a big man.

Seattle still had an NBA team in operation, and Roy hadn't discounted playing for the Sonics, either. Holding the tenth selection, they likely needed to move up in a significant manner to obtain his draft rights. Lucky for Roy, his hometown team wasn't enamored with him enough to make that change. He wouldn't have been home long anyway. Like everyone else in the Northwest, he never imagined that two years later Seattle would be stripped of its pro basketball franchise; the Sonics were moved to the Midwest and became the Oklahoma City Thunder.

Roy's share-himself-with-anyone draft mentality made him attractive to every team in the league, if not infuriated all those so-called pro basketball experts trying to guess the final selection order. When asked for his preferences, he would have mentioned each franchise in the league, if necessary, to get an NBA job. He also noted how his uniform color would remain the same purple shade, from his high school team to college to the pros, if he ended up with the Utah Jazz.

"I won't lie, I'll play anywhere in the NBA," he blurted out with a laugh during the draft buildup. "I'm not picky at all. I would love to play for Utah, Seattle, wherever. It doesn't matter to me. I could be a new Mailman. I've been wearing purple a long time."

Leading up to the June 28, 2006, draft, Portland and Charlotte showed the most interest in acquiring Roy. Trail Blazers' general manager Kevin Pritchard traveled to Seattle and met privately with Roy at Mercer Island's Stroum Jewish Community Center, a location chosen because the suburban gym offered privacy and had a three-point line to test the player's long-range accuracy. The Bobcats coaxed Roy to fly across the country to North Carolina for careful inspection and long conversation.

On a forty-hour trip to Charlotte and back, Roy was surprised that so much time was spent addressing his character, his innermost thoughts, his pristine image, rather than pure basketball stuff. The conversation leaned so much to the personal side that the Pac-10 Player of the Year felt the need to speak up and make sure the Bobcats hadn't forgotten anything.

"They said they were excited about me, because I was a good person and that I was a nice guy," Roy recalled. "I was laughing and I had to ask them, 'But what about my workout?' They said it was fine, that they already knew I was a good player."

Portland's Pritchard arranged to meet with Roy alone on Mercer Island, an affluent Seattle suburb to the east of the city, connected to it only by floating bridge. The Blazers executive preferred to work this way: just him, a prospect, and a quiet gym. This combination allowed him the best opportunity to study the available talent and make a good decision in drafting the right player. Pritchard watched Roy play several times during the season, including the most recent NCAA Tournament. His immediate impression—the guard's athletic ability was greatly undervalued by most scouts.

Unlike his Portland front-office predecessors who collectively gave a teenaged Roy a thumbs-down after a two-hour workout in 2002, Pritchard needed just two minutes in his estimation in the secluded Jewish Community Center gym to become totally sold on the twenty-one-year-old player. The general manager went home and put Washington's All-America recipient and Pac-10 Player of the Year near the top on Portland's draft board.

"In two minutes I could tell he was much more athletic and gifted than you think," Pritchard said. "I thought maybe he wouldn't necessarily be a true point guard, but he'd be an attacker with the ball. With his character and the importance he puts on winning, I think the total package is what makes Brandon as special as he is.

"There are guys who are more athletic, guys who shoot better and guys who do a lot of things better, but with his super competitiveness and willingness to do anything, it was over for me."

Once back in Portland, Pritchard didn't tip his hand to those who wanted to know in the worst way everything he was thinking in remolding the team; in other words, the inquisitive local media. The *Portland Oregonian* newspaper, in its NBA mock draft, predicted the Trail Blazers would choose Gonzaga University's high-scoring forward Adam Morrison with the fourth pick, this after it had Toronto selecting University of Texas big man LaMarcus Aldridge with the No. 1 pick, Chicago taking Louisiana State University forward Tyrus Thomas with the second choice, and Connecticut forward Rudy Gay going to Charlotte in the third slot.

The *Oregonian* concluded Roy wouldn't be taken until the eighth pick, pairing him with the Houston Rockets. This was nothing new for him. At every step of his basketball career, the Huskies guard was greatly underestimated.

However, the Portland paper wasn't totally dismissive of Roy. Consider this thumbnail synopsis of the Washington player: "The most complete player in college basketball. He's strong, can defend, is a leader, can create his shot and is a better shooter than you expect him to be. His stock is rising.

I asked one NBA general manager about Morrison, and the cat steered the conversation to Roy and wouldn't stop talking about him. Right now, people are saying he's in the second half of the lottery, but after some workouts and more exposure, I expect him to be a top five pick in the draft. And I suspect Portland will take a long, hard look at him despite having Martell Webster waiting in the wings. I wouldn't be surprised if this is the player the Blazers end up with."

A few days ahead of the draft, Roy and a large contingent of family and friends traveled to New York to get ready for this life-changing moment. There were assorted media commitments to fulfill and people to visit. Roy and family members met Crawford for dinner. These were still innocent times, too. Leaving his midtown hotel one day, Roy tried to walk the streets and check out the sights, only to get ambushed by autograph seekers ten kids deep. He attempted to accommodate all of them, to the consternation of his waiting father. "I was grabbing him and saying, 'C'mon Brandon!' " Tony Roy said.

The day before the draft, Roy and the other selected players were asked by the NBA to meet with New York reporters and other media members in a fifth-floor ballroom at the well-heeled Westin Times Square Hotel, which housed all of the draft candidates and their families. Sipping on a red vitamin drink, Roy was relaxed and charming. Surrounded by reporters on all sides, he answered a wide variety of questions tossed at him, even the silly stuff, with overly polite and thoughtful replies. What brand of business suit would he wear on draft night? Can he play point guard? Can he play defense? Could he play with Yao Ming? Who was his favorite NBA player? Why did he attempt early entry coming out of high school? Who does his game best resemble? What team would draft him?

Roy said his wardrobe of choice came from a Los Angeles tailor with a French name that he couldn't spell, someone favored by a lot of NBA players and recommended by his agents. Roy said the people scouting him had told him he was interchangeable as a point guard and an off guard, and cited specific input provided by Trail Blazers coach Nate McMillan. Yao, with his towering seven-foot-six size and dominant play, would allow him to develop his game, Roy told the Chinese reporter who asked him.

Kobe Bryant was the pro basketball player he admired most, with Roy kiddingly adding, "I was always a Lakers guy. It would be a dream to play in that system. What star is watching you? Jack Nicholson? Denzel Washington?" Roy said his flirtation as a teenager with NBA early entry was confusing and immature, and that playing college basketball at Washington allowed him to grow up. He said there was not one pro player who he had attempted to emulate in style. He stressed that the strength of his well-rounded game was creating offensive plays off the dribble.

As for his NBA draft destination, Roy offered the following summation to the probing crowd closely pressed around him in the convention room: "There's a real chance Portland. There's a real chance Minnesota. To say for sure that's going to happen, that's too hard. I don't want to set the bar too high and be disappointed."

Too hard? Set the bar too high? Roy eerily had just sized up his upcoming draft-night experience.

Chapter 12

Draft Night

The theater at Madison Square Garden was where the best American amateur and foreign basketball players in the world arrived each June and departed as very rich men. By invitation only, fifteen lucky prospects were summoned to New York, booked into a fancy hotel in Times Square paid for by the league, and permitted to experience the annual NBA Draft firsthand. A sudden lifestyle transformation took place when the commissioner, David Stern, strode to the center podium, leaned into a microphone, and authoritatively called out someone's name. Brandon Roy found out how this feels.

In 2006, Roy was one of the handpicked prospects brought to the "Big Apple" by the NBA and treated to a night that resembled a basketball Disneyland. The theater's front stage, where all of the talent dispersal took place, was dressed up in an elaborate hoop theme. Backboards with rims and nets were fastened to the wall on each side of a centrally located draft board, one that held thirty first-round slots neatly arranged in five rows awaiting names to be inserted. Two metal storage racks on wheels were filled with authentic league basketballs and parked beneath the baskets. The floor was imitation parquet and detailed with white court striping. A circular wooden canopy provided a roof over all of these carefully positioned props.

Left of the stage, ESPN had a makeshift studio set up to provide a live broadcast. Five rows of media seating were stationed directly in front.

Private tables reserved for the players and their families were located to the right. It was enough to make even the coolest player under pressure take a few gulps and feel slightly overwhelmed.

Fifty minutes before ESPN's nationally televised coverage went live, Roy and the others walked onto the stage, all dressed as if attending an executive board meeting, each trying to act casual, but privately churning inside. Garfield High School's soon-to-be-first NBA player wore an elegant black suit with champagne pinstripes, yellow shirt, multicolored tie, handkerchief in his left breast pocket, and clearly a nervous look on his face. The players lined up in two rows for the traditional group photo. Roy stood in the front row, next to Adam Morrison, the high-scoring Gonzaga University forward and fellow Northwest native.

See you in June, Morrison had wisecracked to Roy seven months earlier in Seattle in the middle of their last collegiate game together. This proved to be an insightful greeting for the long-haired scorer from Spokane, though it tipped off his NBA early-entry draft ambitions when the comment was repeated by Roy later to reporters. Everyone now waited several moments for Stern to join them. As he walked up, the commissioner playfully tossed a ball to Morrison. A man stood on a ladder and snapped off several images, and they were done.

Roy made his way to a table set aside for him, sat down alone, and placed a cell phone call. He got up and wandered into a buffet area provided for the players and out of view, more interested in walking off nervous energy than eating. Fifteen minutes later, he was anxiously pacing around the players' cordoned-off seating section, again talking on his phone. Morrison, a diabetic who needed to keep his blood sugar levels under control at all times, sat nearby nibbling on a snack and drinking from a water bottle, also looking frazzled and a little impatient.

Once the players' families were bused over from the hotel and escorted into the theater, a reassuring moment for every player involved, Roy took a seat. This was the one time in their lives that none of these self-assured athletes wanted to be alone. New York's boisterous basketball fans turned up the intensity by noisily entering the building and filling up the seats behind the VIP and press sections.

Sharing Roy's table were his parents, Tony and Gina Roy; his older brother, Ed Roy; his high school sweetheart and soon to become fiancée, Tiana Bardwell; and his sports agent, Bob Myers. Roy had more supporters seated together elsewhere in the theater, a group that included his grandmother, Frances Roy; his sister, Jaamela Roy, and her former husband, Deandre; his best friends, Cole Allen and Lardel Sims; his cousins, Marvin Hall and Saeed Hammond; his AAU basketball coach, Lou Hobson; and his attorney friend, Rich Padden.

"I still think about the NBA draft, sitting at that table," said Roy's brother, Ed. "My eyes were so big."

Back home on Beacon Hill, Roy's aunts and uncles hosted a raucous neighborhood party at his grandmother's house. This gathering drew just about everyone else who had a deep-rooted connection to Brandon Roy and didn't travel with him to New York. Seattle newspaper reporters and TV camera crews who had covered him as a collegiate player also showed up at this address, looking for another story. Even with the man of the hour awaiting his basketball fate some three thousand miles away, this was a party worth attending.

"It was all neighbors, people who grew up with Brandon, people who knew him, and they came over to watch the draft," his aunt Renee Roy said. "There were cars everywhere. That day this street was rocking."

After a half hour of ESPN commentary and preliminary interviews in the TV booth, filler that involved Morrison, but not Roy, it was draft time at Madison Square Garden. In anticipation of the top overall pick, theater fans loudly chanted Roy's name. This was surprising because the Huskies guard was never mentioned as the top guy in any of the mock drafts compiled on the Internet, ESPN, or anywhere else. Roy more often was pegged between the fifth and tenth selections on the lists that rated him the highest. He had been informed that the best big men always went first in the draft; the competitor in him still wanted to know why.

Teams privately registered concern over Roy's surgically repaired right knee and said he didn't appear as athletic as before. Others said he hadn't defined himself as a playmaker or shooting guard, and failed to see the advantage of having that type of multipurpose player. The Atlanta Hawks, holding the fifth pick, concluded they were overstocked at the two-guard position and in their pre-draft meetings had decided to pass on the Washington player.

"They were all talking that I couldn't be No. 1," Roy said, as confident as ever in his basketball abilities and similarly indignant. "I thought, 'Why aren't they talking about me?' They said, 'He's a good player, but he's not a franchise guy.' I said, 'We'll see.' "

Moments later, Italy's six-foot-eleven Andrea Bargnani was the first player taken in the draft, going to the Toronto Raptors. It was hard to distinguish the Madison Square Garden cheers from the jeers. "Who's he?" was a common refrain. The University of Texas's LaMarcus Aldridge, another tall guy, went next to Chicago. He was a more recognizable basketball commodity and received a better reception. The Garden fans once more loudly chanted Roy's name, demonstrating their persistent draft preference. No other lottery pick received such favorable treatment inside the raucous theater. It took a half hour to get through those first five selections: Charlotte settled on Morrison with the third choice, Portland chose Louisiana State University's Tyrus Thomas, and Atlanta picked up Duke University's Shelden Williams.

Attempting to turn around a franchise that had fallen on hard times, the Hawks even had insider knowledge on Roy. Former University of Washington head coach Bob Bender now was an assistant coach on Mike Woodson's Atlanta staff and still a big fan of the Seattle basketball player he had once recruited. He offered everything he knew to the Hawks. The team still couldn't take advantage.

"Our guys liked him but they said, 'What position?' " Bender said. "I thought, 'That's the beauty of Brandon Roy. You don't pigeonhole him.' "

At this point, Stern announced that Chicago's newly acquired Aldridge had been traded, with a second-round draft pick, to Portland, for veteran forward Viktor Khryapa and the recently drafted Tyrus Thomas. This was only the beginning of the Trail Blazers' elaborate draft-day dealings. This was all part of a master plan that included Roy and would be executed flawlessly.

The ESPN studio offered piped-in sound so those in the theater could hear the on-air banter that was directed to the people watching at home.

Chatterbox analyst Dick Vitale described Gonzaga's Morrison as the player in the draft most ready to play right away at the pro level, an assessment from the former Detroit Pistons coach and self-made TV media star that couldn't have been more inaccurate. Roy admittedly was never a big fan of Vitale's, turned off because he felt the bombastic ESPN college-basketball personality had failed to properly do his homework on the Washington player's game. This was an interesting turnabout, with the once grade-challenged Roy getting on someone else for not studying enough.

"I got the label that he doesn't do one thing great, he just does a lot of things good, and I thought that's what makes me a great player," Roy said. "I always felt underappreciated and overlooked. If Dick Vitale had watched me in college, he would have liked me, but he didn't know me. A lot of people slept on me. A lot of people didn't like my talent."

"I didn't know him," fellow lottery pick Tyrus Thomas acknowledged.

At 8:07 p.m. Eastern Standard Time, Roy's turn had come. Stern read out loud that Minnesota had picked him. The pro-Roy theater crowd cheered loudly. Roy stood up, hugged everybody at his table, and with a huge smile pulled on a light blue Timberwolves cap and headed for the stage. After shaking hands with Stern at the podium but curiously finding the NBA commissioner not very chatty at all, Roy was ushered to a back-stage area at Madison Square Garden set up for nonstop TV interviews. A special credential was required for anyone else to gain entry to this behind-the-scenes electronic draft central. Every leading news organization had a broadcast pod set up: ABC, NBC, CBS, ESPN, TBS, and Fox. Drafted players quickly moved from station to station, slipping into a waiting chair, inserting an earplug and bantering with an agreeable TV reporter. It was a frenetic exercise.

Roy sat down with Seattle-based Brian Davis of Fox Sports Net, someone he had known for a long time, and the two started discussing Minnesota, a team that had shown noticeable pre-draft interest in the UW player. Roy seemed satisfied with the Midwest direction in which his basketball career was now headed. Then-Timberwolves coach Dwane Casey was no stranger, previously having worked as a Sonics assistant coach, and he and Roy had huddled together for an extensive pre-draft workout.

"It's going to be great, because I've known Dwane Casey for a while," Roy said in his interview, still looking a little flushed. "I just felt comfortable talking to him. We talked about my high school days. He's a teacher and I'm a student of the game. I knew when he first got the job, it was great for him. He did a great job for Nate McMillan (in Seattle). We just really clicked."

Roy let out a deep breath when asked about playing alongside Timberwolves forward Kevin Garnett, then the cornerstone player of the Minnesota franchise. One of the impressive things about Roy was that while handing out nonstop compliments and pulling stuff off the top of his head, he always had something interesting to say. Being genuine always worked for him.

"He's a superstar in the NBA, and I grew up watching him," Roy said of Garnett. "I know if I can help him out, he can carry the team to great heights. I'm just happy to be part of it. He brings it every night. I'll be happy to first get over meeting him. Once I get over the thrill of meeting him, it will be great to play with him. I don't know what the NBA is all about, but I know if I work hard, I'll make an impact. I'm just happy this is over."

Yet Roy's draft night had not played itself out. Not even close. In mid-answer to a Davis question, he was interrupted by me, a *Seattle Post-Intelligencer* reporter covering Roy's NBA draft experience, and informed he had been traded. That made the Fox Sports interview geared for a Northwest audience suddenly moot and useless, and it came to a stop. The camera and audio momentarily were turned off. Roy was swapped for Villanova University's Randy Foye, who had been drafted one spot behind Roy by the Boston Celtics, and then moved in a multiplayer deal to Portland, before going to the Timberwolves in exchange for Roy. Whew.

Following Roy around in an effort to document all of his draft-night actions at Madison Square Garden, I simply had spotted a bulletin of the trade from ESPN's coverage roll across the bottom of a nearby TV screen and passed along the information. Usually this sort of breaking news comes to a player from a front-office executive, but things were happening too fast in New York for any protocol.

"Portland?" Roy said, looking a little dazed and reflexively removing the Timberwolves cap from his head. "I knew it. I thought that was going to happen when I went up to meet the commissioner and he didn't say anything. Now I'm back on the West Coast, and my parents have to drive only three hours to go to my games. I'm a family man."

Roy then paused for a moment, before asking innocently and to no one in particular, "Does that mean I have to do my media all over?"

Behind the scenes, Portland had worked all day in putting together deals for Aldridge and Roy and had pulled this off. The Trail Blazers entered draft day with the fourth, thirtieth, and thirty-first picks, which weren't going to land them two premium players. They had to trade up, and they likely had to trade up twice. Aldridge was the first priority because he was a talented big man and wouldn't last if Roy went first. The Blazers needed to lock in a deal for the Texas player before working on the second transaction involving the Washington guard. The Roy trade wasn't finalized until an hour before Portland made its first-round pick. Now everything had to go as planned, or one or both deals would be aborted.

These carefully negotiated transactions were contingent on the desired players getting drafted in a projected order and remaining available. There was no guarantee all of this would go down as envisioned. Aldridge seemed a fairly safe bet to stay in the second slot, because Toronto was openly committed to taking Bargnani. Yet there was great concern Roy wouldn't last until the sixth position. Other teams attempted to do what the Blazers had done—move up the draft ladder and land a promising, possibly underrated, shooting guard.

"We knew there was one team hunting and pecking to get up there as hard as they could to get him," Trail Blazers general manager Kevin Pritchard said. "Houston was dying to get up there and get him. I didn't know if we were going to get that trade."

The Rockets, who owned the eighth pick of the draft, told Roy how much they liked him, but ultimately put together a different deal involving University of Connecticut forward Rudy Gay. It was a figurative elbow this time, but not a lasting blow. Houston next shipped Gay and veteran forward Stromile Swift to the Memphis Grizzlies for centerpiece forward Shane Battier. Foye, the seventh choice taken between Roy and Gay by the Boston Celtics, was acquired by the Trail Blazers in yet another prearranged deal, with the idea all along of moving him for Roy's playing rights. How all of this fell into place without added complication and consternation was simply Portland's good fortune.

The Trail Blazers knew all about draft-day disasters. In 1984, a month before Roy was born, Portland spent the second overall pick on University of Kentucky center Sam Bowie, who not only wasn't a franchise savior, but whose presence effectively blinded the Blazers from zeroing in on a much bigger prize that was available: in choosing Bowie, the Blazers passed on a promising University of North Carolina guard named Michael Jordan (he went third to Chicago), whose ultimate contributions to the game of basketball need no explanation. Portland's acquisition of Brandon Roy helped offset that colossal draft blunder a little.

"As soon as [number] five went, there was a huge collective sigh in the building," Pritchard said of learning that Shelden Williams was Atlanta's top selection. "There were definitely a lot of high-fives as soon as we knew we had Brandon."

While overjoyed to stay in the Northwest, Roy later admitted to having mixed feelings about his final destination because the Trail Blazers had acquired Aldridge ahead of him. He wasn't jealous or anything. Yet, rather than go to an NBA team as its No. 1 selection, as he had fully expected, Roy briefly felt like a supplementary pick, almost as if he were a second-round selection. His ego took a momentary beating before he warmed to the idea of coming to Portland in an impressive package deal.

"I talked to my agent and he said, 'You can't feel that way. You have to make them think you're No. 1,' " he recalled.

Quickly gathering himself and redoing the Fox Sports interview, Roy talked about his ready-made Portland connections, of how McMillan would push him to become a better player, of how he and Blazers swingman Martell Webster were Seattle natives who knew each other well and were always meant to play together. He rightfully was more excited about playing in Portland and having the chance to stay in the Northwest, than moving to Minnesota, which was so far removed from his family.

Roy was asked by *Sports Illustrated* reporter Luke Winn how he had learned about the trade. "The *Seattle P-I* broke the story," Roy wisecracked with a smile, nodding to me standing nearby.

Roy was drafted and traded in just thirty-seven minutes. It was a wonder he could concentrate at all and do these rapid-fire interviews. At least he wasn't Randy Foye. The Big East guard was the property of three NBA teams in far less time. Foye walked away with the most impressive draft-night hat collection among his peers.

As Roy maneuvered his way through this back bunker of TV cameras, he ran squarely into Gay, the Connecticut forward with whom he had briefly scuffled in his final college game three months earlier. The players hugged each other. They shared a few pre-draft workouts together, so this wasn't a first-time greeting since their double technical foul. By now, all was forgotten from that overheated moment in the NCAA Tournament. "I got traded," Roy told him. As he continued down the busy hallway, the former Washington player allowed himself a moment to reflect about Gay and their controversial postseason play and the ramifications. "We probably would have been in the Final Four if that hadn't happened," Roy said in a wistful manner. "We're friends now. Once you meet the guy, you like him."

Leaving the makeshift TV community behind, Roy went around a corner and plopped down in a dark interview area set aside for the print journalists covering the draft. Before taking the first question, an NBA official seated next to Roy barked at him to put on his team hat, which apparently was standard marketing protocol for this moment. "I got traded," the player said once more, this time with a shrug.

Once this media exchange was started, Roy was asked about the marketing advantages of a Northwest player joining the Portland franchise. His inquisitor apparently was unaware of the intense and often hostile college rivalry between the bordering states that made this situation a little more complicated than it might have appeared on the surface. Roy briefed him with a short yet poignant response that offered a Northwest olive branch.

"I played a lot of games in Oregon, and hopefully they won't boo me too bad, and they'll grow to like me," he said.

Roy took a few more questions. He felt good about the draft. He was an NBA player now, and recognized it was a much tougher game to play. He talked about living up to everyone's expectations, including his own. He got up and went looking for his family entourage.

Nearly an hour after Roy's name had first been called, Stern stepped to the podium and announced the player's trade to Portland. This news drew a mixed response from the now-subdued theater crowd, mainly because it wasn't breaking news. Clearly it wasn't something just making the rounds in the VIP section, either—Roy's family members already clutched Trail Blazers hats while waiting for him.

"I thought somehow I'd be in Portland," Roy concluded as he left the press area, still holding the Timberwolves cap. "I wonder if I can keep this hat?"

As the draft activities started to wind down, Roy and his family left Madison Square Garden, climbed into a couple of limousines, and drove off to celebrate at a Manhattan restaurant. Roy and his entourage, which briefly included Aldridge, next visited entertainer Jay-Z's 40/40 Club, an upscale sports bar and lounge on West Twenty-Fifth Street. Roy sat in a VIP section, too weary to do anything but watch everyone else intermingle. His sister cut him a piece of strawberry cake, his one big indulgence for this life-changing moment in New York. Everybody was giddy in his group. The second son overnight had become an NBA player and a multimillionaire, automatically receiving a contract deal worth $5.4 million over two years, with a two-year option. He had picked up a talented big man in Aldridge for a teammate, though they would need more time to get better acquainted.

"I didn't really know Brandon," Aldridge said. "I was in the South and he was in the Northwest. I just knew of him."

The following morning, Roy's family members grabbed an extra-early flight for home, a trip that required a stop in San Francisco. Everyone was totally exhausted by the time they reached the Northwest. With just two hours of sleep, Tony and Gina Roy talked of getting back to their West Seattle rental unit and taking showers. The city was hot and sweaty when they landed. However, their long, transcontinental journey had taken them from the NBA good life and brought them back to harsh hometown reality.

When the Roys pulled up, the front door to their home was disturbingly cracked open. Someone had broken in and helped themselves to their belongings. A TV, computer, and some cash were missing. Tony Roy found one of two new suits that Brandon had purchased for him discarded in the backyard. The bedroom was ransacked. Another TV was moved but not taken. A side window was broken. Luckily, Brandon's basketball keepsakes were safely tucked away at his grandmother's home, which was protected at all times by an alarm system, not to mention the nonstop family and friends congregating.

Feeling violated by this intrusion of their thirteen-year rental home and still badly in need of a shower, the Roys booked a local hotel room for the night. They suspected a neighbor with a known drug problem had burglarized their place, someone fully aware the house was occupied by the family of aspiring NBA player Brandon Roy, and that everyone had gone to New York. They didn't wait around to find out. "We never went back," Gina Roy said.

Brandon heard about the Delridge break-in much later. That morning, he was headed to Portland. He was scheduled to leave on an earlier flight than his Seattle-bound family members. After exiting the 40/40 Club, he said good-bye to everyone, grabbed his travel bag, and took a car service to the airport, instantly falling asleep in the backseat on the way. The driver had to wake him when they reached the drop-off area.

It was 4 a.m. and the John F. Kennedy International Airport gates were still locked. Once inside, Roy saw Aldridge checking in and heading to Portland, but traveling on a different airline. The overly fatigued Roy fell asleep once more, sprawled over a couple of airport seats, after learning his flight was delayed. Somehow he woke up and made it to Oregon. He endured two days of media interviews and meetings with Trail Blazers personnel in his new NBA city before he flew back to Seattle. Roy, with arms crossed, and Aldridge, holding a ball in his left hand, were posed together for a *Portland Oregonian* advertisement that read: "Meet the lottery picks everybody's talking about."

Roy was exhausted, but his dream, the one he had shared in the fifth grade with Nate Robinson, the one that proved tempting but unattainable while finishing up the twelfth grade, and the one that needed to be rescheduled when he suffered his knee injury as a Washington junior, had finally come true. He was a full-fledged pro basketball player.

CHAPTER 13

ROOKIE OF THE YEAR

Brandon Roy would be a much better pro than college player, his AAU coach told him. He had unique basketball instincts that were more suited for the NBA. He was perfect for this game. Roy didn't believe him.

Yet, once introduced to basketball's big leagues, Roy felt totally liberated as a player. Rather than adjust his style, he was finally allowed to do what felt natural. Everything about the highest level of basketball suited him. He learned that everything his summer coach Lou Hobson had envisioned for him was true.

While the collegiate game moved at a faster pace and was controlled by the coaches, Roy was instructed by Portland Trail Blazers coach Nate McMillan to set the tempo on the floor, no matter how orderly and deliberate, and to make his own decisions. The rookie guard was dumbfounded by how well this system worked in his favor.

Now Roy touched the basketball on every possession. He had so much more freedom and power on the court, he kept checking with McMillan to make sure he was reading the situation right. Roy freelanced on a pick-and-roll play and scored, and later felt compelled to ask his coach if he could do that more often, just dribble up and score rather than pass first. McMillan probably had to keep from laughing.

"I liked it when I got into the NBA," Roy said. "Nate rolled me the ball and said, 'Do what you do.' He didn't try to control me. He let me play. It was, 'Make the best play you can.' I thought I was going to be pretty good in this league. I told my dad, 'I'm going to be a pretty good player, I can feel it.' "

This was everything the graceful athlete had dreamed about as a basketball player. This was so different from his first three years at the University of Washington, which required a continual adjustment of his game to suit his teammates and deal with a knee injury. It ran counter to what University of Arizona coach Lute Olson had envisioned for him. Roy didn't have to ask for any of this court autonomy now. It beckoned him.

"Even in college, those were Nate's teams, and that was Nate's style and Will's style," Roy said, referring to former Huskies teammates Robinson and Conroy, both eventual NBA players who thrived on a scrambling, up-tempo approach. "I did the best I could to win, but that wasn't my style of game. We played more my game as a senior. I'm not a pickup game player."

"We used to run up and down the floor so fast, Brandon used to say, 'We need to slow this down a little bit,' " said former teammate Bobby Jones, who went on to play for eight NBA teams.

On November 1, 2006, "Welcome Back," the theme song created by John Sebastian for the 1975-79 hit TV sitcom *Welcome Back, Kotter*, played softly over the public-address system at Seattle's KeyArena before the Portland-Sonics season opener as the players came out of the locker rooms for warm-ups. This musical selection drew an immediate smile from Roy, the person for whom this customized reception was intended. He was in a strange place, yet a familiar place. He was making his NBA debut and he was doing it in his hometown. This was a Wednesday night in the city and opening night of the 2006-07 season for the league's two Northwest members. A sellout crowd of 17,072 was on hand, many of them eager to cheer for the former Washington standout again.

Clay Bennett was in the house, also qualifying as an NBA rookie. The Oklahoma City businessman was prepared to watch his first regular-season game as the Sonics' new owner, at this point telling everyone in town that the franchise wasn't leaving Seattle for the Central Time Zone. It wasn't clear how many people believed him.

Yet this night belonged to Roy. He had earned a starting job for the Trail Blazers in the preseason. He had forged a new playing identity, wearing

No. 7 now, because it was a combination of his and his brother's Garfield numbers; No. 3 was already worn by veteran Portland player Juan Dixon. Roy was given the chance to play his first regular-season professional game under the best circumstances possible. He liked the way everything fell into place for him.

"That was like a fairy tale," Roy said. "I had been to KeyArena a few times as a spectator. Now I was the show."

Everything was great up to tipoff. All Roy had focused on was playing in Seattle again. Yet with the ball ready to be tossed up, reality sank in, followed by an unexpected case of jitters. He might have overlooked something in his game preparation—it was time to perform at basketball's highest level, to show that he belonged, and he might have let that responsibility slip a little.

"At the tip, I'm thinking now I've got pressure on me to play good," he said. "I hadn't even thought about that."

Roy was able to readjust his thinking. His first time out, he scored twenty points, connecting on ten of sixteen shots, and drew raves as he helped Portland pull out a 110-106 victory. At halftime, McMillan called him aside and reminded him to relax in front of the home crowd, which he did. He initially had been a little starry-eyed in trying to create floor space against veteran Sonics guard Ray Allen, someone Roy knew well—Roy had played against him in summer pickup games at the University of Washington— and whose game he greatly respected. With his coach's encouragement, Roy found a nice second-half rhythm and his first pro game was a success.

Roy would later enjoy huge and heroic scoring nights, postseason and All-Star nights, but there was no greater satisfaction for him than starting his first night as a professional basketball player on a positive note.

"I was back at Garfield High School," Roy said. "When I walked off, it was honestly the best moment of my NBA career."

Nothing could ruin his opening night. Not even the cell phone call he received from girlfriend Tiana Bardwell as he was about to board the chartered jet Blazer One that would whisk him and the team to Oakland for the next game. She drove his Cadillac Escalade sports utility vehicle to the opener, parked it in a fenced-in lot in the bustling lower Queen Anne neighborhood, and found it burglarized after she returned from watching him play at KeyArena. Welcome back? How about please give it back? Roy normally would have been upset. He just shrugged it off after hearing that his SUV was broken into and stereo equipment and music were taken. He told Bardwell to call their insurance company, report the damage and loss, and move on. "I was so happy the way the game went, it couldn't bother me," Roy said. "Three days later, I said, 'Tiana, where did you park?'"

Three nights later, Roy made his Trail Blazers home debut a success, too, supplying sixteen points in an 88-86 victory over his original NBA destination, Minnesota, at the Rose Garden Arena. He finally got to meet the imposing Kevin Garnett, though it wasn't necessarily the warm and fuzzy exchange he had proposed on draft night when he was momentarily a teammate.

"He gets in my face and it's, 'Boy, you're weak,'" said Roy, thrilled just the same to be insulted by the Timberwolves superstar. "It was, this is Kevin Garnett. He's going to push and shove and try to intimidate me. A year ago, he didn't even know I existed."

While starting out smartly in the first week of the season, Roy's pro career didn't unfold exactly or as smoothly as planned. Over the first twenty-five games, Roy and fellow rookie LaMarcus Aldridge were never on the floor together, which was not by design. They were the franchise building blocks, yet hadn't had a chance to bond. They were touted as a lethal inside-outside combination that would work well as a team within a team, and be in place for years to come after the significant horse-trading that transpired to acquire them on draft night. They were kept apart by injuries for nearly the opening third of their rookie season.

Aldridge missed Portland's first six games while recuperating from offseason shoulder surgery. As soon as the rookie from the University of Texas was declared fit and ready to play, Roy was ruled out with an inflamed left heel, missing nineteen consecutive games and twenty of twenty-one overall. The first-year guard landed awkwardly in practice and his heel became increasingly inflamed and painful. He pulled on a protective boot and decided to rest the affected foot rather than submit to surgery. A doctor proposed shaving down an intrusive talus bone causing the discomfort. Roy's choices were to miss a month or more of games without invasive action (he eventually was out six weeks) or sit out half the season after the surgical procedure, which was unacceptable to him.

"I was home watching the games," Roy said. "I didn't want people to forget about me."

While sidelined, Roy was denied his first opportunity to play against each of the league's biggest headliners, Kobe Bryant and LeBron James, as their teams came and went on the Trail Blazers' schedule. Roy's favorite player throughout college and high school was Kobe Bryant, after his early fascination with Michael Jordan ended with the latter's retirement. Tiana bought him that Kobe jersey to wear when he was at Garfield.

With the Lakers visiting Portland, Roy was mesmerized by his first close-up view of Bryant, even while sitting there in street clothes. In college, he and Conroy had purchased three-hundred-level KeyArena tickets and talked Washington coach Lorenzo Romar into letting them out of their afternoon practice early; they watched Kobe play from a considerable distance. Now Roy sat courtside, intently studying the elite player's every move before and during a game the Trail Blazers would win 101-90 without him.

"I watched the way he warmed up, the way he stretched, the way he approached the game, how he took his shots," Roy said. "I thought this was going to be fun, sitting in the front row, so close to someone I respected and looked up to."

Not as much fun was the bag-carrying duty expected of all Trail Blazers rookies on the road. Roy was not exempt. Veteran players exited the charter bus and headed straight for their hotel rooms, instructing their first-year teammates to bring their late-arriving luggage to them. This meant Roy, as well as fellow rookie LaMarcus Aldridge, often had to sit in the outside chill with the Portland equipment guys until 2:30 or 3:00 a.m., waiting for a rental truck to arrive with the players' essentials. Once he picked up his load of assigned bags, he next had to locate a room list—because none of his teammates left him any clues—knock on hotel doors and deliver the goods.

Portland forwards Jamaal "Big Cat" Magloire and Zach Randolph abused Roy the most with this hazing practice. Randolph at least slipped the rookie a

$100 bill or paid for an ensuing dinner for his services. Magloire offered only a curt "thank you." When Roy casually mentioned he was a starter, playing a lot of minutes, and needed his sleep, the Big Cat, who was a reserve, not pulling enough game time to suit him and more rested than he wanted, only sniffed and informed Roy that rookies don't get tired.

Dealing with older teammates was one thing. Playing against hometown friends was another. On January 3, 2007, Roy and the Trail Blazers hosted the New York Knicks, whose roster included his Seattle buddies Jamal Crawford and Nate Robinson, though Robinson was forced to sit the game out as part of his ten-game suspension for a brawl against the Denver Nuggets involving several players. Crawford, Robinson, and Roy expressed great sentiment in this moment, fisticuffs the absolute last thing on anyone's minds. The guys from the neighborhood were pro players together for the first time. They had arrived. They laughed and joked before the contest. They didn't say a word to each other during the action.

Crawford dropped in twenty-five points, some of it at the expense of Roy, who scored fourteen, and helped lead his Knicks team to an easy 99-81 victory at the Rose Garden. The Trail Blazers rookie had let their close friendship get in the way of his play, and that couldn't happen again.

"It was hard for me to get in the game competitively," Roy admitted. "It was me and Nate and Jamal in the NBA? I thought it was cool. Coach took me off Jamal and put Ime Udoka on him; he thought I was playing him too nice. At that moment, I said I was always going to attack it after that. But it was hard to see them as opponents."

Even more difficult was trying to stop Kobe Bryant at full throttle. On March 16, 2007, the league's showcase player went off for sixty-five points, hitting twenty-three of thirty-nine shots, while leading the Lakers to a 116-111 overtime victory over the Trail Blazers at the Staples Center in Los Angeles. This was the second-highest scoring total of his career, sixteen points shy of his most explosive effort against the Toronto Raptors a year earlier. Kobe wasn't cocky when he was spectacular, just super confident. He didn't talk trash, just game-time facts. In one exchange, he drove into Roy, spun off him hard, went up in the air for the shot, and yelled out "Bucket!" as he let go and the ball whistled through the hoop.

This was Roy's third encounter with Kobe. Roy had previously watched that victorious first meeting from the bench, then helped the Trail Blazers upset Bryant and his team 112-108 in Los Angeles. Apparently, the Lakers standout decided enough was enough in dealing with Portland. The Blazers were looking at their first season sweep of L.A., but Bryant made sure that didn't happen.

"I guarded him some, but I wasn't the main guy," said Roy, who scored just fourteen points that game. "I thought everybody's going to think Kobe got sixty-five on me. The coach said that's what great players do, is will a win. I thought that's what I'm going to do some day, is will a win. We also decided we would take more pride and Kobe better not score more than thirty against us [after that]."

These were all rookie lessons that had to be learned. Roy was a conscientious student now. He was seeking only the highest basketball grades in the NBA, and he tested well. In the second month of the season against the Toronto Raptors, he put together his first double-double performance at the pro level (16 points, 10 rebounds). In January, he had a double-double (19 points, 10 rebounds) against the ultimate competition, the Cleveland Cavaliers and LeBron James. He also supplied double-doubles against the Denver Nuggets (22 points, 11 assists) and Washington Wizards (19 points, 12 rebounds). In the final month of the season, he dropped a career-best 29 points on the Utah Jazz. He became increasingly efficient, surprisingly so for a newcomer. As the season started to wind down, Roy began drawing attention as a serious Rookie of the Year candidate.

"I saw him play at Washington and I knew he was going to be a good player, though you just never know how things are going to transpire, but he was so strong and in control," said Mike Bibby, then an Atlanta Hawks guard and former Pac-10 player from the University of Arizona.

"You could tell he was going to be good off the bat," Trail Blazers center Joel Przybilla marveled. "One thing is he went to four years of college. You could tell that definitely benefited him."

The compliments kept coming. Veteran opponents such as Sam Cassell, then a member of the Los Angeles Clippers who retired shortly thereafter, impulsively told Roy to his face he was a great player. Boston Celtics coach

Glenn "Doc" Rivers pulled the Trail Blazers guard aside and confided to him that Rivers was making his high school-aged son Austin watch tape of Roy because he wanted the younger player to approach the game the right way, just like the rookie. Roy was far more advanced and unselfish as a basketball player than anyone had imagined.

"I think the best players in the league know who they are, and they are themselves every day," Portland general manager Kevin Pritchard said. "They don't do something else. It's not in their character profile. We always said Brandon, as he profiles out psychologically, is the caretaker. He likes everybody to feel good, everybody to understand, and everybody to be involved. He has that innate caring ability for everyone."

Although intrigued by Roy's talent, Atlanta Hawks forward Josh Smith offered this cautionary thought about his well-rounded game, "He's a great player and a great leader, but I think sometimes he's a little too unselfish."

As good as it was, Roy's debut NBA season didn't end with a flourish. After playing in fifty-seven games, fifty-five as a starter, or twenty-four more than his longest college season, he felt wear and tear catch up to him. He sat out the final three games of the regular-season schedule with left knee tendinitis. His team finished 32-50 and was never in playoff contention at any time.

Roy's only real joy as his first Trail Blazers season played out was the March 2007 birth of Brandon Junior, making him a father for the first time. He was in the delivery room in Seattle when his son was born and actively involved in bringing the new arrival who carried his name into the world. Changing dirty diapers was now part of this NBA player's ever-changing lifestyle. "Everybody said I did a good job, but it was a real experience," Roy said of his son's birth.

Two weeks after the close of the regular season, Roy was voted NBA Rookie of the Year and given the Eddie Gottlieb Trophy, named after one of pro basketball's founders and pioneers. There wasn't much mystery to it. Roy drew all except one of 128 first-place media votes, with the lone dissenter a Toronto Raptors broadcaster named Chuck Swirsky, who ironically had grown up in suburban Seattle and learned his trade in Roy's hometown, but felt no hometown allegiance in this matter. At the time, Roy was heard to grumble about his good fortune, though it had nothing to do with Swirsky's ballot. Even after averaging 16.8 points, 4.4 rebounds, and four assists per game, Portland's first-year guard didn't feel he deserved this sort of individual attention—he didn't win enough with the Trail Blazers.

"I'd never accepted an award without my team doing well," Roy explained. "That was tough. Here I was watching the playoffs, and my team was not in it. I'd always been in the postseason. They said if you see the players who have won the award, you'll be happy about it."

Besides, no other NBA rookie was more deserving. Reviewing the top 2006 draft selections, Roy outperformed, by a wide margin, each of the five players chosen in front of him, and all of those behind him. Toronto's Andrea Bargnani, the top overall draft pick and Swirsky's curious choice for Rookie of the Year, averaged 11.6 points and 3.9 rebounds per game while starting just two games. Aldridge, Roy's Portland teammate and the second pick overall, supplied nine points and five rebounds an outing, starting only twenty-two times.

The other three players drafted in front of Roy, Charlotte's Adam Morrison, Chicago's Tyrus Thomas, and Atlanta's Shelden Williams, each struggled and failed to make much of an impact with their teams. Morrison and Williams eventually washed out and were moved elsewhere, considered NBA busts. Even Randy Foye, who was acquired by the Trail Blazers and traded for Roy, his second trade on draft day, was traded yet again.

"Brandon always had a good screen-and-roll game," Morrison said while relegated to deep sub for the Los Angeles Lakers, rarely stirring from the bench, after his trade from the Charlotte Bobcats. "What makes him so good is he's a legitimate six-five or six-six and he could pull up. I always figured he would be a great player in this league."

Roy took another look at the NBA Rookie of the Year honoree list and started to warm to it. The honor roll included Michael Jordan, LeBron James, Tim Duncan, Allen Iverson, Jason Kidd, Vince Carter, Shaquille O'Neal, Larry Bird, Kareem Abdul-Jabbar, Oscar Robertson, Wilt Chamberlain, and Elgin Baylor—very exclusive basketball company. The Trail Blazers had offered up just two previous Rookie of the Year award recipients, guard Geoff

Petrie (1970) and forward Sidney Wicks (1973), and then none for the next thirty-four seasons.

Upon further review, Portland's latest Rookie of the Year decided he shouldn't feel so guilty about accepting this award. It would come in handy in future contract negotiations. It was historic. It also seemed only right that an NBA trophy identified by the acronym ROY should go to a player named Roy. He allowed himself to revel in the moment.

"I thought maybe twelve years down the road I'd be happy about it, but here was Jordan, and he held this trophy, and Tim Duncan held this trophy," Roy pointed out. "After another one hundred years of NBA basketball, people will look back and see I was Rookie of the Year, and that's amazing to me."

CHAPTER 14

AN ALL-STAR

Brandon Roy's second season in Portland hardly seemed worthy of any rewards or accolades when it started. The Trail Blazers lost nine of ten games early on. At the end of the downturn, Roy had suffered through one of his worst spells as a pro player, at least when healthy, scoring just ten, eight, and four points in consecutive losses to Indiana, Dallas, and San Antonio. Veteran forward Zach Randolph had been traded to the New York Knicks in the offseason and opponents were gearing their defenses toward Roy at every opportunity, and he hadn't adjusted to this increased attention. Worse yet, the insinuation was made publicly that Roy had urged the team to move Randolph elsewhere, and this unpleasant rumor trailed him into the season. He had been forced to address it internally with his former teammate.

"That upset me," said Roy, offering a flat denial that he carried any influence in Randolph's departure. "Me and Zach are friends. He asked me about that. He called that morning. He said, 'People said you wanted me traded.' I told him that was the farthest thing from the truth."

The second-year guard helped Portland pull an immediate turnaround, rattling off thirteen consecutive victories. Roy played some of his best basketball in December 2007. During the NBA's longest winning streak of the season to that point for any team, the Trail Blazers knocked off, in order, Memphis, Miami, Milwaukee, Utah, Golden State, Utah, Denver, New Orleans, Toronto, Denver, Seattle, Minnesota, and Philadelphia. Roy did a little of everything as his team took off. He outscored the Heat's Dwyane Wade 25-21. He connected on 11 of 13 shots against the Bucks. He tossed a double-double effort at the Nuggets, collecting 26 points and 11 assists. He came close to a triple-double against the Jazz, stringing out a 25, 9 and 8 stat line, just missing in rebounds and assists.

"It felt like we couldn't lose, didn't matter who we played," Roy said.

The uninterrupted Portland success, however, finally came to an end with a 111-101 loss in a return match at Utah on December 31, 2007. The Trail Blazers then rattled off four more wins, giving them seventeen in eighteen games. The shorter victory run ended at Toronto, but not because of Roy. He scored a career-high thirty-three points against the Raptors and added ten assists for his seventh NBA double-double, though it wasn't enough to prevent a 116-109 double-overtime loss.

In the midst of all of Portland's positive play, Roy was invited to sit for a taped postgame interview with TNT basketball broadcaster Cheryl Miller and explain the Blazers' newfound success. They touched on his NBA success, his struggle at the University of Washington in obtaining a qualifying test score for admittance, and even his previously stated aversion to tattoos and gold chains. He explained once more how he didn't need to look or dress similar to someone else to make it as a successful NBA player, that he was a humble guy who needed no frills. To which Charles Barkley, back in the studio, remarked, "I like him more now."

Roy was named Western Conference Player of the Week on consecutive weeks, December 9, 2007, and December 16, 2007. All-Star talk suddenly was everywhere he went. McMillan used this as a motivator, telling his young guard to keep playing hard, to make it difficult for the coaches not to choose him when the time came. Roy tried to stay detached and ignore the increasing speculation surrounding him, to no avail.

"I was so lost in the moment, I'm not thinking about those accomplishments," he said. "People started to whisper, 'Brandon Roy might be an All-Star.' It was, 'No, not now.' "

But the more people brought up his All-Star possibilities, the more Brandon warmed to the idea. He was lying on his bed at his suburban Portland rental home, waiting for all the votes to be tabulated and wondering if he had enough, when word was delivered. He next did what every self-respecting, first-time NBA All-Star selection would feel compelled to do at a time like this.

"I ran around the house for twenty minutes, screaming," Roy said.

His successful NBA debut in Seattle was arguably his most gratifying moment, signaling his arrival at the game's highest level, and his NBA Rookie of the Year award was reassuring, further validating his talent level. Yet his inclusion in the 2008 All-Star Game in New Orleans was his most emotional moment as a pro player.

After Roy was finished with his spontaneous victory lap and celebratory yodel, he called his parents back in his hometown. His mom cried. They reflected on his long and sometimes arduous journey to reach this basketball pinnacle. They reminded each other how just three years earlier Roy had been a reserve as a college player coming off arthroscopic knee surgery and not on anyone's draft boards. Now in his second NBA season, he had been designated as one of the league's twenty-four elite players, one of the twelve best from the West.

"That was the first All-Star Game I ever played in," Roy said, referencing all levels of basketball. "I wasn't even a McDonald's All-American."

When the final teams were unveiled, Roy was one of seven Western Conference reserves selected by the league coaches. After all the screaming had subsided at home, he had become the first Portland player to receive an All-Star invitation in seven seasons, since forward Rasheed Wallace in 2000-01. He was the first Trail Blazers guard selected in fourteen seasons, since guard Clyde "The Glide" Drexler in 1993-94. After missing those twenty-five contests to injury as a rookie, Roy had barely played a full season of games in the NBA to this point and he now was designated as one of the league's elite players. His Portland coach wasn't surprised at all about the second-year guard's rapid ascension through the league.

"Brandon is talented and people thought he had talent, but he's worked hard to get where he's at," McMillan said. "If you put forth that effort, good things happen."

Roy later took bows in front of an appreciative gathering of a few hundred fans at the Rose Garden. He drew the voters' attention by rescuing the Trail Blazers from disaster and restoring franchise calm.

Roy's place in the NBA universe was rubber-stamped by veterans throughout the league. Denver Nuggets forward Kenyon Martin, whose University of Cincinnati team was emulated by Roy's Garfield High School team, was among those impressed right away by the newcomer. "He's an exciting player, a great player in this league, because he's always working hard to get better," Martin said. "He listens, and that's half the battle."

To earn his All-Star Game spot, Roy beat out well-deserving Utah guard Deron Williams and Golden State guard Baron Davis in the coaches' balloting. The Trail Blazers backcourt player was one of three first-time West selections, joining a pair of New Orleans newcomers, forward David West and guard Chris Paul. This annual midseason honor is an elite club that doesn't always have a lot of openings; all twelve East players were repeat selections.

Normally never one in need of personal reward or reaffirmation of his basketball talent, Roy badly wanted this individual NBA prize. All of the cascading attention had made him a believer that he had reached another level in his play, and he was ready for confirmation. He was so into it now, he could recite facts that demonstrated how unique this moment was. Roy pointed out how Dwyane Wade and Chris Paul had been NBA Rookie of the Year recipients before him, but were unable to land All-Star spots in their second pro seasons. Roy understood how receiving this basketball honor was similar to landing a big movie role after previously handling only bit parts. Anything but a trip to New Orleans would have been difficult for him to accept.

"I would have really been disappointed if I wasn't an All-Star," Roy said.

In his next Portland game, Roy celebrated his selection by coming up with his first triple-double at any level of basketball. He did it against close friends, too. On February 1, 2008, he collected twenty points, ten rebounds, and eleven assists in a 94-88 overtime victory over the New York Knicks at the Rose Garden. It all came down to a rebound that he fiercely wrestled away from anyone who got in his way. Seattle buddies Jamal Crawford and

Nate Robinson were in the opposing lineup. His parents were in the crowd. It was a cherished milestone to tuck away. Even in defeat, his friends were rooting for him to keep doing wondrous things.

"I don't think anybody can duplicate B-Roy," said Robinson, an unwavering supporter. "He's good now, but he had that knee surgery. If he had never got hurt, they would have been talking about B-Roy like they do Kobe and LeBron. He can jump as high as anybody in the NBA. He has hops like Vince Carter. He's one of the smartest players I ever played against. He's unbelievable, man."

Larry Brown, a head coach for ten NBA and ABA teams, was in charge of the New York Knicks when Roy started to emerge brilliantly on the college level, and Brown learned about the Washington player much like he would a stock tip. The coach's initial interest in Roy came down to locker-room talk.

"Nate used to talk to me about Brandon all the time, so I started following him and I became a big fan," Brown recalled.

Two weeks later, Roy headed for New Orleans and double duty at the All-Star Game. He competed in Saturday's Rookie Challenge and Youth Jam, coming up with seventeen points and seven assists for a collection of the league's second-year players, who defeated the rookie team 136-109. In an unusual move, Roy wore a red headband in support of his Rookie Challenge teammate Rudy Gay. Formerly rivals, Roy decided to show solidarity with him—Gay was looking for someone to wear a headband so he wouldn't be alone with this look. However, Roy removed the headband during the first timeout because it felt uncomfortable.

Roy spent the rest of his time in New Orleans wandering around an unfamiliar pro basketball landscape full of bright lights. He noticed nearly everyone else had patches on their All-Star warm-ups, signifying their previous selections, not unlike travel stickers on a piece of luggage or a car bumper. He was one of the few players who had none. He was the only second-year player invited to Sunday's showcase event. The game's greatest players didn't know him personally, and he admittedly wasn't sure how to act in their presence. For the most part, he sat quietly in the locker room and spoke only when spoken to, taking it all in.

"I felt I was a generation ahead of my time," Roy said, surrounded by heroes as well as peers.

One of Roy's most memorable moments came at practice when West teammate and Lakers superstar Kobe Bryant impatiently yelled at him, "Cut through! Cut through!" Roy did his best to appease his one-time basketball hero. He was happy to be noticed and eager to oblige. The experience was all so surreal, he and Kobe playing together. He had fantasized about this moment leading up to the NBA Draft. He had dreamed about it in high school while he wore that souvenir Bryant jersey. Yet the real thing proved far more challenging than he had expected.

"I could play against Kobe and Tim Duncan, but to be on their team made me so nervous," Roy said. "I didn't want to let them down. There were so many league MVPs on my team. Kobe came into the league in 1996, and I was twelve years old then. Now I was on the same team with him."

Acceptance didn't take long, though Roy was an unknown for the league's more established players. It was just a matter of getting acquainted. "I didn't know what to expect of him," admitted Dirk Nowitzki, a Dallas Mavericks forward and perennial All-Star selection. "I didn't see him in college. I don't watch college. He just kept improving and improving and improving, and became one of the best two guards in the league."

Roy had nothing to be worried or ashamed about in Louisiana. He held his own with the great ones. In an entertaining 134-128 loss to the East, the Portland player topped his team in minutes played with twenty-eight and finished tied for the scoring lead with Denver's Carmelo Anthony and Phoenix's Amar'e Stoudemire, all three with eighteen points. His mother sat in the stands and cried when he entered the game, and cried again when he hit his first shot. He connected on eight of ten attempts, two of three from three-point range. His other miss was a one-handed dunk attempt off a Paul lob pass that bounced off the back rim, but was still spectacular for its degree of difficulty.

With Bryant making only a cameo All-Star Game appearance after tearing a finger ligament, Roy played far more than he expected. He was also surprised to be in at the end, with the game close and a lot of the big-name players seated on the bench, but he made the most of this first opportunity in the NBA spotlight.

The kid from West Seattle now had universal respect throughout the basketball world. What made Roy great was still hard for everyone to pinpoint. Everywhere he went, the guard continually turned around some of the best players in the NBA and made them look helpless as they tried to keep up with his series of clever head fakes, intermittent hesitations, and quick first steps. Former high school and college teammate Anthony Washington used to say that Roy had a move for every defense. Others suggested the Portland guard's unique maneuverings closely resembled a baseball change-up pitch, and that in uncanny fashion he knew exactly when and where to increase and decrease his speed.

"Brandon is one of those very good athletes who play in slow motion," Denver Nuggets coach George Karl said. "I kind of like players who play in slow motion. They have a better chance of getting faster. Those guys tend to be better team players."

"He has kind of like an old-school game, not too flashy but very effective," said Tyrus Thomas, who became a Charlotte Bobcats reserve forward after he was taken two spots ahead of Roy in the 2006 draft by the Trail Blazers and traded to the Chicago Bulls. "He's not the fastest guy and he's not the quickest guy, but he manages to use what he has to be effective."

If he were a boxer, Roy would have made his living as a counterpuncher, bobbing and weaving before responding. His intent was to react in a calculated manner on the floor to whatever his opponent did. Go one way, and he headed in a different direction. It wasn't all that complicated. It was mostly instincts and good choices.

"I see the game before I make a move," Roy explained. "That's why I play slow, because I'm thinking it out before I do it. Players try to force me to do things. I *want* you to make me do things. If you sit back, I'm a little lost. I say one guy shouldn't be able to guard me. I'm not one of the quickest guys, but I'm one of the sneakiest. I lure you to sleep, and then boom!"

No one turned their nose up at Roy or tried to belittle his unique playing style, something that very easily could have happened in such an ego-driven sport, particularly with a new kid seeking everyone's acceptance.

More often, NBA players were appreciative of what he did, claiming they played like him or wishing they could play like him.

"Him and I are similar," said Denver Nuggets guard Chauncey Billups, a five-time All-Star. "I pretty much play in my own speed. It's about changing gears. It's about changing speed. He's kind of methodical that way."

Dallas Mavericks forward Shawn Marion said of Roy, "It's nonchalant, but he's really savvy. He's got his own speed. It's a savvy style. I like it."

The Blazers improved to 41-41, but missed the 2008 playoffs once more. Roy, who sat out eight games with assorted injuries, averaged 19.1 points, 4.7 rebounds, and 5.8 assists per game, all notable increases from his rookie season. In his sixth game on the schedule, he scored a career-best thirty-two points against the Mavericks in a 91-82 victory in Dallas, later exceeded by one to establish his scoring best in his trip to Toronto, making him a very resilient road player. Most of all, his floor leadership impressed everyone wherever he went. He turned in eight games that season with assists in double digits, twice dishing out a career-best twelve, both coming in home victories over the Lakers and Kobe.

Yet after another long NBA season, Roy experienced noticeable wear and tear. In August, he underwent arthroscopic surgery to deal with a partial meniscus tear in his left knee, the same one that had been repaired once before when he was at Garfield and the same one that made him sit out at the end of his Trail Blazers rookie season. The surgery took Roy back over the Columbia River—the Washington-Oregon state line—and was performed by Dr. Don Roberts, the Trail Blazers' team physician, at the Washington Regional Medical Center in neighboring Vancouver.

Roy had plenty of reasons to get healthy. With his third NBA season approaching, it wouldn't be long before the guard would be running around the house, yelling and screaming his head off again.

CHAPTER 15

FIFTY-TWO POINTS

Brandon Roy noticed something different in warm-ups. His shot felt great. His body felt great. In his words, he felt "bouncy." Everything was working at the highest order. It was almost scary how it all came together.

On December 18, 2008, before going back out to face the Phoenix Suns at home in a nationally televised game on TNT, Roy's pregame checklist was so overwhelmingly positive he turned to longtime Trail Blazers trainer Jay Jensen and said he expected to have a big night.

Roy had no idea it would be this big: he piled up a career-high fifty-two points in a 124-119 victory at the Rose Garden, marking only the fifth time a Portland player had reached or surpassed the half-century mark in scoring in thirty-eight seasons. It was just two points shy of Damon Stoudamire's franchise record in 2005. It was the second-highest total in the NBA at that point in the season, trailing only Tony Parker's fifty-five points for the San Antonio Spurs. Kobe Bryant, LeBron James, and Dwyane Wade later would surpass Roy with sixty-one, fifty-five, and fifty-five, respectively.

Always capable of scoring, Roy convinced himself it was detrimental to the team, even in his third season in the league, if he strayed from his all-around offensive game and put up huge scoreboard numbers. His previous NBA best was thirty-eight points, just six nights earlier at home against the Los Angeles Clippers. As if to illustrate his point, the Trail Blazers lost that game 120-112 in double overtime.

Yet, against the Suns on his highest-scoring night, all of Roy's points were needed to guarantee a positive result in a highly competitive matchup worthy of a national viewing audience and Marv Albert's raspy play-by-play description on TNT. Roy scored 11 consecutive points for his team in one stretch, 14 in a row in another. He connected on 14 of 27 shots from the field, 19 of 21 from the foul line. He surprised himself with how often and how easily the ball went into the basket.

"I'd never scored forty before," Roy pointed out. "I only scored fifty because we had to have it. If Phoenix would have stopped, I would have stopped. It was big shot after big shot. Every shot was needed. I got into such a rhythm. I never had confidence like that in my life."

Roy pulled up on a fast break and hit a jumper, a shot he normally wouldn't take. He connected on a fade-away jumper, one that came with a high degree of difficulty. He moved around the perimeter easily sinking shots as if he were alone in an empty gym. He was good on five of seven three-pointers against the Suns. His confidence ballooned with each ball that went down. His coaches told him to keep shooting. On this night, it didn't matter how much or how far.

The Rose Garden crowd roared its loudest and shouted "MVP! MVP! MVP!" after Roy put his team ahead for good on a three-pointer with 1:01 remaining, breaking a 119-119 tie. At that moment, the guard thought anything was possible.

"This was my night," Roy said. "I just felt I couldn't be guarded, and they put everybody on me. It was special. From the moment I warmed up, I thought it would be a great night. But a great night for me was thirty-five points."

"You almost expect him to do this night after night," Portland coach Nate McMillan told reporters afterward.

From his Rose Garden midcourt seat, Portland general manager Kevin Pritchard did a serious double-take when he glanced up at the scoreboard early in the fourth quarter and saw Roy's point total rapidly turning over as if it were green ticker-tape numbers on a bull market run on Wall Street. The front-office executive was used to his third-year guard quietly compiling a hefty stat line during each game. This sudden outburst bordered on the ridiculous, for how quickly the numbers multiplied.

"I looked up at the board and he had forty-two, and it was, 'Are you kidding me? That's got to be an error. There's no way he has forty-two points already!' " Pritchard said.

With a sellout crowd of 20,650 squeezed into the arena, teammate Martell Webster was injured, in street clothes, and couldn't find a seat anywhere on or around the Portland team bench. He settled for a spot in a sound booth next to video coordinator and assistant coach Kaleb Canales. From his secluded vantage point, the idled guard watched Roy's individual outpouring with great fascination.

"I thought every shot was going in," said Webster, who grew up with Roy in Seattle and knew what was possible from him. "Until that point, we'd been waiting for him to do something like that. Even if he didn't want it, the ball was in his hands."

It all made sense. That week, the entire NBA was tattooed at the offensive end by Seattle, player after player. The geographic assault on the rim was breathtaking and all inclusive. The impish Nate Robinson got everything started. On a Tuesday night in Los Angeles, he came off the bench for the Knicks and dropped thirty-three points on the Lakers and Kobe Bryant, no small feat for a guy used in a reserve role. "I'd seen what Nate did," Roy confirmed.

On Thursday night, it was Roy's turn, with his career scoring effort coming at the expense of a formidable Suns lineup that featured Shaquille O'Neal, Amar'e Stoudemire, Steve Nash, and Grant Hill. "You can't let a guy go for fifty-two," Shaq lamented in the locker room. "It's not acceptable." It wasn't preventable, either.

On Saturday night, Jamal Crawford, Roy's buddy now with the Golden State Warriors, cut loose for fifty points on the road against the Charlotte Bobcats, two off his all-time NBA high. Three nights later, suburban Seattle product Rodney Stuckey of the Detroit Pistons put up a career-best forty points at home against the Chicago Bulls.

Over one scoreboard-assaulted week, ending two days before Christmas in 2008, it was guys from Rainier Beach, Garfield, and Kentwood high schools, taking turns in the league spotlight with unabated scoring displays. They momentarily turned the NBA into the Northwest Basketball Association, if not a Seattle parks and recreation league. They casually strolled into the different arenas at basketball's highest level and treated them as if they were the Rainier Vista Boys and Girls Club, Mercer Island's Stroum Jewish Community Center, or the Kent Commons Recreation Center, their offseason workout halls at home where the points always flowed freely.

"It was the Seattle flu going around," Robinson wisecracked, proud of his hometown heritage that now offered a surplus of high-scoring talent passing through the league unchecked.

It was an amazing display of condensed firepower. In and out of the starting lineup that season, Robinson even chipped in forty-one points two months later, still four shy of the NBA career best he had turned in during the 2007-08 season against the Trail Blazers and his good friend Roy. These guys always had their fifth-grade game faces on whenever in each other's company. Meantime, Crawford became just the fourth player in NBA history to score fifty or more points for three different teams (joining Wilt Chamberlain, Bernard King, and Moses Malone), after earlier coming up with fifty-two for both the Bulls and Knicks. Stuckey demonstrated his offensive creativity by ringing up his forty-point total with just one three-pointer converted among his assemblage of shots.

Not to be outdone, Seattle native Aaron Brooks, a second-year Houston Rockets guard, saved his career-best pro point total for the playoffs later that season—on May 10, 2009, Brooks cut loose for thirty-four against the Lakers and Bryant. Veteran Dallas Mavericks guard Jason Terry, yet another Seattle native, twice scored thirty-three points that season, as a starter against Sacramento in January and as a reserve against Washington in March, which was five points off his NBA best.

Yet Roy's offensive showing was the one that everyone talked about. Normally his versatility and well-adjusted ego wouldn't permit him to have a fifty-two-point night—at any level of the game. He felt guilty the first time he scored thirty in college, concerned he had hogged the ball against UCLA, when he should have hogged it more during a five-point road defeat as a sophomore. After all, he connected on twelve of eighteen shots that night against the Bruins. He came up with thirty points by halftime of a summer AAU game, yet pulled himself out of the contest early in the second half to give others a chance to play, even with those same teammates imploring him to go for fifty or sixty points. He settled for forty-one. The most he had scored for the Washington Huskies was thirty-five, accomplished in back-to-back home games against the Pac-10's Arizona schools. Now Phoenix was scorched by a rare and quintessential moment of Roy individuality. His friends throughout the league were captivated by it.

"I watched every play," said Robinson, who sat mesmerized in front of a TV set in New York. So did an equally attentive Crawford on the road in an Atlanta hotel room. Text and phone messages crisscrossed the country that night once Roy's last point had sizzled through the net. Nearly everybody in the league who originally hailed from Seattle wanted to share in this moment, if not comment on it. Or respond to it.

"Brandon's was different than mine," Crawford said. "His was on national TV. He called me and said, 'Big brother, I got one, too.' The next night I had to do it again."

"I was taking a nap that day and my phone kept ringing," Roy said of Crawford's high-scoring reply. "It was just like me and him playing every day in the same gym. Now we both were getting fifty."

The fifty-two-pointer capped a prolific stretch of scoring for Roy, his most abundant in the NBA to that point. He had consecutive games with thirty, thirty-three, thirty-eight, twenty-nine, and fifty-two points. To reiterate his team concerns, the Blazers lost three of those five.

"I've always thought if I score thirty we can't win," he explained in a way that made sense. "In college, I scored big against Arizona and we lost. I'm always trying to figure it out. Scoring is not for me. I don't want to be someone who scores a lot and doesn't win."

His next time out, Roy was limited to just eight points by Denver, which swarmed him with defenders. He actually played against the Nuggets in consecutive games in this stretch. Both times he faced two and sometimes three players crowded around him. Roy, who scored nineteen in the second game against the Denver team, was more curious than concerned about this increase in defenders as opposed to his decrease in scoring. He asked

Denver center Kenyon Martin on the floor why the sudden emphasis on him? Professional respect was the answer. "We saw every one of those fifty-two points you had and we're double-teaming you everywhere," Martin told him.

There was just one problem with this defensive plan. In their third season together, Roy and the six-foot-eleven Aldridge had grown increasingly comfortable together in moving through the league. Aldridge, a young power forward and Dallas native, now offered a solid offensive option to Roy. Portland general manager Kevin Pritchard and his scouts Michael Born and Chad Buchanan had envisioned all of this happening when sizing up the 2006 NBA draft. They saw two mobile, confident athletes who could mesh well together, and the Trail Blazers did everything possible to obtain them.

"I thought they would both be phenomenal pick-and-roll guys," Pritchard said. "If you were going to build your team around great kids, you wanted them hardworking, and both are, and you wanted them unselfish, which both are."

"I was in awe to play with such a talented and legitimate big man," said Roy, who went without one throughout his college days at Washington. "With Bobby [Jones] and Mike [Jensen], we were always undersized at the U-Dub. We started talking about becoming the John Stockton and Karl Malone of the Northwest Division."

In turning the Trail Blazers into a playoff team during the 2008-09 season, Roy and Aldridge learned to play off each other in a highly effective manner. They came up with twenty-four games in which both scored twenty points or more. If you stopped one, you probably weren't going to contain the other. The franchise was hoping this was the rollout of a ten-year plan.

Roy was still Portland's main man. During the opening week of the 2008-09 season, he hit a turnaround three-pointer from thirty feet under heavy guard at the buzzer to beat Houston 101-99 in overtime at the Rose Garden.

"It was just a hell of a shot," Rockets forward Tracy McGrady, one of two defenders lunging at him, later told reporters. "He just went up there, caught the pass, and [hit a] seventy-footer." In early February, Roy did it again with the final seconds ticking down, only from much closer range.

He drove the middle, hung in the air, and dropped in the game-winner as time expired to topple the Knicks 109-108 at home.

Between last-second heroics, Roy had a lot of personal things to deal with. In January 2009, his daughter, Mariah Leilani Roy, was born in Seattle. A few weeks later, Roy returned to his hometown to have his number 3 jersey retired at the University of Washington.

Number-wise, Roy was the Huskies' Babe Ruth, an athlete with game-changing greatness only without the old-time baseball player's checkered background and bulging waistline and ego. He showed up with several family members for a heartfelt pregame ceremony before the Huskies beat USC 78-73. As he held Brandon Jr. in his arms at midcourt, Roy watched as a sheet was lifted off his number in the rafters, just the second jersey retired by the school, joining Bob Houbregs's number 25. It made Roy emotional, marking another career highlight and providing him with an unexpected public landmark on his inspiring basketball journey.

"When I was here, I was dreaming of making big shots to help us win, or I'd dream of winning a national championship," Roy told reporters. "But having my jersey retired never crossed my mind."

Not long after that, Roy was rewarded with his second consecutive All-Star Game selection. He was headed for Phoenix this time. At a news conference, he shared with beat writers how the Trail Blazers' Pritchard had sent him the following text message: "Don't shoot to be one of the best; be the best." While enjoying the moment, Roy made sure to mention Aldridge when addressing the media gathering about receiving a repeat reward, careful to protect their valued basketball partnership. "I'm looking forward to having LaMarcus here, and Greg [Oden], and that will come," he said diplomatically.

Once in the desert, Roy was no longer the anonymous NBA star. This meant he was much more comfortable with his fellow All-Stars and now totally unnerved by the fans drawn to his growing celebrity. In the West locker room, both Shaquille O'Neal and Kobe Bryant, who were reunited with coach Phil Jackson for the first time since their nasty split as Los Angeles Lakers, chatted up Roy and playfully poked at his son, Brandon Jr. "Let me see little B-Roy," Shaq said. "Hey, little man," Bryant said, reaching for the toddler. They were Roy's heroes while he was growing up. He had to remind himself again that these guys were now teammates and equals for the weekend. "I'm a fan, and I'm sitting next to Shaq," Roy said.

For the second consecutive year, Roy brought family members and friends with him so everyone could share in the All-Star excitement together. However, it proved much harder for Team Roy to hang out in Arizona than it had been in Louisiana. Roy innocently tried to meet his personal entourage for lunch in the hotel lobby, was swarmed by pushy well-wishers and aggressive autograph hounds, and had to run for cover. He was forced to sneak out a back way of the hotel from then on to meet with his relatives.

"He got swarmed," said Jaamela Roy, his sister. "It was wonderful. It was sweet. That was my brother. He likes to hang out with us so he can be himself, be silly, and make jokes, and not be the celebrity. I think of him being the basketball player when I see him on TV; when I'm around him, he's still my brother."

"I don't think it's set in that he's this type of person, because he doesn't act like that," Ed Roy said of his brother's widespread celebrity. "But it was fun going to the All-Star Game and shaking Alonzo Mourning's hand and seeing LeBron James standing right over there."

For part of his Phoenix stay, Roy was back in the fifth grade again. On Saturday night, he watched as Robinson, his hometown buddy and consummate showman, come out for the dunk contest dressed in a fluorescent green New York Knicks uniform with matching shoes and elbow sleeve, while trotting out a green basketball. Robinson, always the ultimate showman, outdid the Orlando Magic's Dwight Howard to capture the first of what would be three NBA dunk titles. It was kryptonite against a player who advertised himself as Superman, and the miniature force of nature won.

The next day, Roy had a much easier time getting on and off the court than he did walking through the hotel lobby. In a 146-119 victory over the East, the Trail Blazers guard once again drew high marks for his all-around play. He topped his team again in minutes played with thirty-one minutes and tossed in fourteen points, sinking seven of eight shots, and adding five rebounds and five assists. People now had come to expect this sort of thing from Roy, especially on a big stage.

"When we play him, the coach says, 'What do you know about this guy?' " Robinson pointed out, referring to his Knicks days that ended when he was traded to the Boston Celtics in 2010. "I say, 'Coach, there is nothing you can scout about this guy. You either have to double him or hope he has an off night.' "

"He doesn't do crazy stuff to show off, or take crazy shots just to shoot," said Boris Diaw, then a Charlotte Bobcats forward and Roy's former 2002 tryout partner in Portland. "He's very precise. He takes very good shots. He's one of the toughest guys in the league, for sure."

There were no more pro basketball firsts for Roy, outside of winning an NBA championship. He was Rookie of the Year, an All-Star, a fifty-two-point scorer, and a playoff participant. He was comfortable as a pro player, and the league was comfortable with him. He still did things his way, sharing himself to the point of exhaustion.

On a March night in 2009, Roy walked onto the Rose Garden floor for pregame shooting. Tip-off was still more than two hours away. This typically was the most selfish time of the game-day routine for the unselfish Trail Blazers guard, because all he did was catch and shoot and get lost in this repetitive exercise. Roy, however, didn't launch a jump shot until he first acknowledged everyone around him in the near-empty arena with a wave or nod: Utah Jazz players, team employees, media members.

As Roy made his way to the far end of the court, the Blazers dance team practiced a new routine at midcourt. The Aerosmith song "Sweet Emotion" wailed over the public-address system. Technicians scurried around checking out TV and radio equipment. The black and red arena seats were empty. Everything was in preparation mode, including Portland's top player.

For twenty minutes, Roy deftly worked his way around the perimeter, using his huge hands to catapult balls over the outstretched arm of a team attendant and smoothly into the basket. When he missed a long-range jumper, he blew on his hands and fiercely rubbed them together as if this would be enough to warm up his shooting touch. And then he was done, at least with his basketball responsibilities.

Roy spotted me in the stands, and wandered over and engaged me in conversation, wanting to know why his hometown Sonics had been hijacked to Oklahoma City. He turned to find Utah guard Deron Williams waiting to speak with him and obliged this opposing player, though it was someone who would bump and shove him for the next couple of hours. He spent a few easy moments near the team bench with Portland assistant coach Dean Demopoulos, discussing something that made him laugh.

On his way out, Roy was stopped by a Trail Blazers public relations official, who pointed to the end zone, mentioned the word "client" and asked for a favor. This person in the dark suit didn't have to plead for it, either. Roy chatted up a man and his young daughter and signed an autograph for them before he disappeared into the locker room to get ready for the game. Serving as the on-call goodwill ambassador had become part of his Trail Blazer job description. He fulfilled a role that was never hard for him.

"He's a throwback player," Demopoulos said. "I liken him to the old players like Oscar Robertson and Walt Frazier. He does whatever is necessary. This kid is the best. He knows people. He takes time to get to know you. He just knows how to communicate."

The Trail Blazers did their best to promote him. Roy's likeness covered a sixty-foot-high poster hanging down the outside wall of an inner-city parking garage, posed with his hands on his hips, left foot balanced on a basketball and serious expression on his face. An image of Roy also was the central figure of another mammoth promotional advertisement that covered most of a building near that parking garage, flanked by the waist-high images of the Trail Blazers' Aldridge and Greg Oden. This montage of young players delivered the following message to Portland fans: "Rise With Us."

After the All-Star break, Roy and Aldridge led Portland into the playoffs for the first time in six years, finishing off a satisfying 54-28 regular season. Oregon's largest city was ecstatic that the franchise had come all the way back from its law-breaking and losing ways with heroic, low-maintenance players. The Trail Blazers didn't last long in the postseason, eliminated by Houston in six games, but they gave an encouraging preview of what the future might hold. Against the Rockets, Portland's top two players combined for fifty points or more three times. In a 107-103 victory in Game Two, they were at their best together; Roy poured in forty-two points while Aldridge backed him with twenty-seven. They collectively connected on twenty-six of forty-six shots. Together they snatched nineteen rebounds.

Houston's defensive stopper Ron Artest, always good for a controversial quote, was ridiculed everywhere in the media when he told a TV interviewer during the playoff series that Roy was the best player he had faced that season. What about Kobe? What about LeBron? Artest defiantly held out that Roy was still the best. Reporters either were too busy poking fun at Artest or found him surly and fed up with them thereafter unwilling to offer further detail about this bold statement, leaving it unexplained publicly. Only Roy received the full answer when his competitive and outspoken Rockets opponent pulled him aside.

"I know that Kobe is going to score and other guys are passers, but I couldn't read what you were going to do," Artest informed Roy. "You were so hard to predict. You were the hardest guy I ever had to guard."

Roy and Aldridge had come to Portland in reverse order. The big man was considered the more valuable draft pick. The situation now had sorted itself out in a different manner, and no one was complaining. The new pecking order had Roy on top in terms of priority, though these players were never too far apart in offensive production. Roy led the 2008-09 Trail Blazers with a 22.6 scoring average, ranking him tenth among the league leaders, while the willowy Aldridge supplied 18.1 points per game. They had a fluid court presence together. It was still hard to believe that the Trail Blazers had pulled both of these guys out of the top six in the same draft. It was front-office genius.

"I like him as a teammate," Aldridge said of Roy in 2009. "Portland did a good job of stealing him from Minnesota. He's the face of the team and the franchise."

Brandon Roy, age seven, is a serious-minded cyclist
at his grandmother's Beacon Hill home in Seattle.

Brandon strikes a Heisman Trophy pose while playing with his cousin, Brandi Roy.

Brandon, age eleven, stands (in front of the man wearing a white shirt and tie) with his 1996 American Athletic Union Click basketball team. Brandon and teammate Aaron Brooks, second to the left of Brandon, both would play in the National Basketball Association one day.

Clockwise, from top left, are Brandon's fourth-, sixth, eighth-, and ninth-grade school photos

Brandon looks for a shot in the Class 4A Boys' State Basketball Tournament at the Tacoma Dome in 2000.

Brandon attends the 2002 commencement at Garfield High School in Seattle, sharing the milestone experience with his grandmother, Frances Roy.

Brandon dated Tiana Bardwell in 2004 when he was a University of Washington sophomore and she was a Garfield High senior.

His tongue seen in the style of Michael Jordan, Brandon dribbles up the floor during a University of Washington Husky game in the Alaska Airlines Arena in November, 2005.

Letting go of their emotions, Brandon and Husky teammate
Bobby Jones bump chests in jubilation at a UW home game on
New Year's Eve, 2005.

Only two jerseys have been retired in more than ninety years of Husky men's basketball. Brandon's No. 3 hangs in the Alaska Airlines Arena rafters with Bob Houbregs' No. 25.

A tuxedo-clad Brandon Roy attends an NBA function
with his father, Tony, and mother, Gina.

Fifth-grade buddies Nate Robinson of the New York Knicks and Brandon Roy of the Portland Trail Blazers hang out before playing their first NBA game against each other.

Brandon and Tiana were proud new parents
of their first child, Brandon Roy Jr., in 2007.

Capping his first pro season, Brandon Roy, above, receives the 2007 NBA Rookie of the Year award. He is accompanied by Portland Trail Blazer coach Nate McMillan and general manager Kevin Pritchard.

Brandon with two prized possessions -- his infant son and his NBA Rookie of the Year trophy.

The Roy Family, from top, left to right: Brandon's mom Gina holds Mariah, Brandon's daughter, and is seated next to Brandon's brother, Ed; Brandon's sister, Jaamela Roy, holds Ed's son, Kane Roy, and her own son, Roy Robinson; and Brandon holds his son, Brandon Jr., and Ed's daughter, Jordan Roy; Ed's son, Marquise Roy, and a cousin, Deoncie Jarvis, join the others in the front row

Brandon's growing family: son Brandon Junior, wife Tiana, and daughter Mariah.

Brandon and Tiana hang out during some down time
at the Rose Garden in Portland in October, 2010.

Brandon goes through his pregame warm-up routine before a home game.

Brandon runs the floor like a greyhound
in a Portland Trail Blazer home game.

Easily bouncing the ball, Brandon gets the Portland offense started.

Brandon signals a play to his Trail Blazers teammates.

Always media friendly, Brandon awaits the start
of a TV studio interview in Portland.

Brandon Roy is besieged by young admirers
during a school visit in May, 2007.

Brandon tries his hand as a school crossing guard
in Portland in September, 2006.

Comfortable in the big spotlight, Brandon dunks
at the 2009 NBA All-Star Game in Phoenix.

Brandon sits on the Portland bench between teammates
Patty Mills, left, and LaMarcus Aldridge, right.

Leaving Phoenix's Steve Nash behind, Brandon dribbles
into the key in an October, 2010 game.

Brandon tosses up an off-balance jumper over the Suns' Steve Nash.

Demonstrating his versatility, Brandon drives to the basket for a left-handed lay-in, beating the Suns' Jared Dudley.

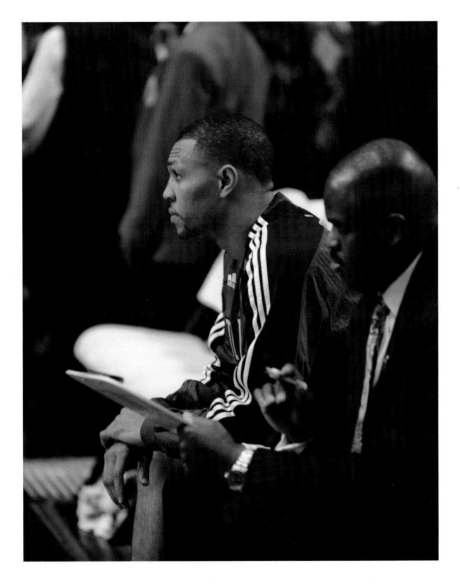

Portland coach Nate McMillan and Brandon watch the Blazers
wrap up a win in October, 2010.

Brandon drives on Marcus Thornton of the Sacramento Kings (23) in his first game with the Timberwolves.

Brandon shoots over Sacramento's James Johnson (52) in Minnesota's 2012-13 season opener.

CHAPTER 16

MONEY PLAYER

An exciting yet unpleasant part of the NBA is the money involved. While it might seem that the league just throws the green stuff around, the truth is all niceties disappear when player compensation is up for renewal. After a contentious 2009 summer of negotiations, Brandon Roy received everything he wanted in finalizing his second contract with the Trail Blazers, except an expedited deal.

For collecting all of his individual awards and bringing the team an overdue playoff appearance in his first three seasons, Roy somewhat naively reasoned that Portland would reward him with the $83 million extension his agents requested without drawing things out. He learned this was still very much big business, and that no one willingly hands over the kind of contract terms he was seeking without offering some perfunctory resistance. He never sat at the bargaining table, but the daily updates supplied by his agents kept him on edge for several weeks.

The two sides argued over length of contract, not rate of pay. Roy wanted a four-year deal, with an option for a fifth. The team stubbornly offered one fewer year across the board and wouldn't budge. Roy's representatives laid out his track record of instant NBA success and a deep-rooted connection to the Trail Blazers fan base. The team pointed to his previous injuries and a tough economy that had cut into ticket sales, and so it went until this stalemate was broken.

Roy always had the upper hand in this offseason bartering. It would have been lunacy not to sign him. Concerned his top player might be getting alienated by his first exposure to the highly impersonal negotiating process, with his rookie contract automatically prorated by his draft position and prearranged by the league's collective bargaining agreement, Trail Blazers president Larry Miller took him to lunch midway through the dealings to keep things civil.

"You have to be selfish, and I don't know how to be selfish," Roy said. "It was tough. It was up and down. It was more disappointing that the Blazers didn't want to commit to me more. It wasn't just business to me. I really cared about this team. I wanted them to care about me. My biggest thing was, 'What are we arguing here, guys? I thought as a player I'd done everything I could. What am I negotiating?' "

The team's final contract argument came down to giving Roy all of this money and then watching him become complacent and lose his motivation. It had happened to other NBA players before, the Trail Blazers pointed out. It was a fruitless debate. Roy didn't resemble anyone else in the game with his versatile, selfless style, and the team knew that. His representatives reminded the negotiators across the table that Roy always played basketball in a conscientious manner, and he was committed to doing it for Portland whenever he was on the floor.

In early August of 2009, after three months of intense discussion, Portland general manager Kevin Pritchard called Roy, who recently had turned twenty-five, and informed him the deal was done on their end, that Trail Blazers owner Paul Allen was pleased to have him under contract for five more years. They still had to iron out the amount of money that would be paid up front, versus how much would be deferred. The new contract wasn't revealed to the Portland news media for another four days while minor details were settled. It was just the beginning of the Trail Blazers locking up their designated pillars of the franchise. Two months later, the team agreed to a five-year, $65 million extension for forward LaMarcus Aldridge. Different from the 2006 draft order, with Roy now considered the more valuable player, his welfare had to come first this time.

Roy's predetermined rookie contract stood to jump from $3.9 million in its fourth and final year to $14 million in the first year of the new deal, not a bad raise at all. His two NBA contracts totaled nearly $100 million. That represented a lot of Swedish Fish. That easily could have covered the rent for a lot of homes along Delridge Way. He could have bought another Ford Taurus, if not a fleet of them. It was a step up from his past paydays of ironing clothes, cleaning out those noxious shipping containers, and washing luxury rental cars out of public view. "I think he still has that money [in a shoebox]," Tiana Roy said only half jokingly.

This commitment also seemed to signal that Roy was serious about becoming the rare modern-day NBA player who could spend his entire career with one franchise, a fact not ignored after everyone reached the contract agreement. "He is one of the unique players to have a chance to have that sort of relationship with one team," Bob Myers, Roy's sports agent, confirmed while revealing the finalized deal to the Associated Press wire service for nationwide distribution.

One thing the Trail Blazers couldn't question or try to spin was Roy's widespread popularity in Oregon's largest city, and throughout the state. During negotiations, basketball fans and newspaper writers called for the team to sign him no matter what the cost. Portland had always been a slow-paced town, and Roy was the ideal combination of athletic talent and impeccable personal history for this upstanding environment. If his predecessors were the Jail Blazers, he was the warden, keeping the peace.

"I love the kid as a person," said Pritchard, who was fired following the 2009-10 season and left knowing that his draft acquisition of Roy was his finest Portland moment. "He's been great to me. We've had some issues, but I'd do anything for him."

All Pritchard had to do was walk through the Rose Garden on any given game night and count how many people were wearing a red, white, or black jersey, printed or stitched with a No. 7 and Roy's name. It was possible that more families gathered together for Trail Blazers games than anywhere else in the NBA, and there was visual evidence in the arena that more of those fans wore Roy's number than any other Portland player's. A typical Trail Blazers fan was Scott Randolph, a Hillsboro resident and purchasing agent for an electrical contracting company. He was dressed in a bright red Roy jersey for no other reason than good citizenship carried a lot of weight with him.

"I grew up being a fan of players like Walter Payton, guys who exemplify what it means to be a good human being," said Randolph, referring to the Hall of Fame football player while seated in the stands with his three foster sons. "I've always been a guy who roots for players who are upstanding in the community. Brandon carries himself very well. He's a gentleman off the court."

People of all races, genders, and ages have come to the Rose Garden dressed in Roy gear. For a 2009 exhibition game against the Denver Nuggets, the player's followers included multiple couples on dates outfitted in matching Roy stuff, along with a guy with tattoos and facial studs, a radiologist, African-American women, Asian-American men, bearded men, pubescent girls, and teenager Chris Lenartz, son of Blazers public-address announcer Mark Mason, all attired in No. 7. Susan Cheever, an unemployed, middle-aged woman from suburban Wilsonville—able to find just enough money and energy in an economic downturn to purchase a red Roy jersey and a game ticket—came to watch him play, for no other reason than her admiration for his clean-cut image. "He seems so down to earth and he's a family man," Cheever said.

Roy said all that money wouldn't change him at all, but he noticed other people were now acting far differently toward him because of it. He wondered who among them would still care about him if didn't have such a big bank account. He was careful when it came to building new relationships.

"Now I'm not going to act like I don't enjoy it," Roy said of his riches. "I like to fly first class. I like nice cars. But as far as my attitude, and how I treat people, it hasn't changed me. The biggest difference I noticed is people feel a sense of entitlement when they have money and lose a sense of values. People around me started to change. I'd notice when people would lobby to be close to me. When I was twenty, people weren't breaking down my door to be my friend."

With Roy and Aldridge each signed to rich, new contracts, and center and former No. 1 pick Greg Oden healthy, the Trail Blazers were poised to take the next step from rejuvenated playoff qualifier to serious championship contender in 2009-2010. True to his negotiating word, the much richer Roy was ready to play and was never more productive when his fourth NBA season tipped off. In the preseason, he demonstrated a leadership role, calling out whiny Portland teammates in a stern yet tactful manner, telling them to quit complaining and imploring them to bond together before the real games began.

In two of his first three games to open the season, Roy scored thirty points against the Denver Nuggets and came up with a season-high forty-two points against the Houston Rockets. Of course, Roy's long-standing reluctance in assuming a more accelerated scoring role for his team proved true once more—Portland lost each game. The Trail Blazers were a little out of rhythm early in the season, but everyone figured it wouldn't take them long to find it.

These hopeful feelings, however, lasted for a quarter of Roy's fourth season before they took a serious hit. A December 5 home game against the Rockets proved both exhilarating and depressing. In the 90-89 victory, Roy drove down the lane and sank the game-winning shot with 3.2 seconds remaining. Yet the Trail Blazers lost the services of Oden, who crumbled to the floor in the first quarter, fracturing a kneecap while attempting to defend guard Aaron Brooks, the Seattle native and Roy's schoolboy opponent. Oden, who seemed more mobile and confident manning the middle of the key during his brief playing stint, was done for the season.

Roy and the Blazers tried their best to keep it together. The guard recorded the seventeenth double-double performance of his NBA career, and his only one of the season, against the Sacramento Kings at home, picking up twenty-five points and ten rebounds in a 95-88 victory. In a nationally televised game on Christmas day, Roy dropped forty-one points on Denver and got a rare positive team result with his big numbers on the holiday stage, a 107-96 victory. A week later, he scored thirty-seven against Golden State and survived this point overindulgence once more, sharing in a 105-89 win.

The following week, Roy led his team to a 107-98 victory over the Lakers and Kobe Bryant, handing Los Angeles its ninth consecutive defeat in Portland and giving his favorite player far more fits than adulation. Roy came up with 32 points, 6 rebounds, and 5 assists. Bryant responded with 32 points, 8 rebounds, and 7 assists. It wasn't much of a standoff, though. The ever efficient Roy took just 11 shots, sinking 9, to reach the shared scoring total while Bryant needed 37 attempts, hitting 14.

A difficult Trail Blazers season, featuring one crippling injury after another that gutted the roster, turned especially exasperating for Roy on January 13. During a 120-108 victory at home over the Milwaukee Bucks, he came up lame in the opening half. He had suffered a severe right hamstring muscle injury and had to sit out the rest of that game. He missed fifteen of Portland's next sixteen games, even returning home to Seattle for the latest blood-flow therapy to speed his recovery. Worse yet, he received his third All-Star Game selection but had to skip the show in Dallas in order to recuperate, which was a lot like picking the right lottery numbers and receiving no payoff whatsoever. There was plenty of space on his living room wall to hang another jersey, too.

"I always loved his game when he was at Washington and I thought he'd be a great player," said Dallas Mavericks center Brendan Haywood, who went to school at North Carolina. "Now that he's been a three-time All-Star, I still didn't think he'd get there this quick. I love what he does for that team."

Roy's health started to desert him just as he elevated himself to his highest level as an NBA player. The website SI.com, in releasing its 2010 midseason report, listed the following as the league's top five players: Cleveland's LeBron James and Dallas' Dirk Nowitzki at forwards, Orlando's Dwight Howard at center, and the Lakers' Kobe Bryant and Roy in the back-court. In this instance, even if it was no more than one Internet site's idle musings, this meant that the Trail Blazers' guard had surpassed the likes of Miami's Dwyane Wade and Phoenix's Steve Nash in stature, relegating them to the second team.

"Top five in the NBA, that's crazy," Roy said. "That put a smile on my face."

Shortly after the All-Star break, Roy returned to action, stiff and hesitant as he tried to run the floor. This led some in print to suggest that he should blow off the rest of the season and not risk further injury. Eventually, the protests died down, the hamstring loosened up, and the Trail Blazers guard resembled his old self. On March 11, he scored forty-one points in a 110-105 victory at Golden State. It was his fifth career NBA game of forty points or more. Roy was 4-1 in those highest-scoring outings, which tested his negative-team-impact theory some. As it was, broken down, the Trail Blazers won comfortably whenever he scored more than thirty-nine points, but were decidedly average (9-10) when he scored in the thirties.

Roy still wasn't completely healed, but he played through it as best he could. Eight days later, Roy connected on just four of eighteen shots against the Washington Wizards, missing fourteen consecutively at one point. But he made his last one, sinking a twenty-two-foot jumper with a bare .09 of a second on the clock to secure a 76-74 victory—the fourth last-second, game-winning bucket of his NBA career.

After securing a second consecutive playoff berth, Roy and the Trail Blazers watched their patchwork season tested by the unthinkable. He suffered another knee injury, his fourth as a basketball player—two on each weathered joint—dating back to his Garfield days. On April 11, during the last week of the regular season, Roy was playing defense when he became entangled with the Lakers' Ron Artest at the Staples Center. He twisted awkwardly with Artest standing on his foot and felt his right knee, the same one that he injured in college and had delayed his pro basketball career, give way. He suffered a partial meniscus tear that would require arthroscopic surgery. He missed the final two games of the regular season. He bravely held out hope the swelling and pain would subside and allow him to return for the start of the playoffs.

"I want to play," Roy told reporters at a Rose Garden news conference a day later. "It's the playoffs. You play eighty-two games and you take a beating just to get to these moments, and I want to be out there."

However, Roy agreed to surgery five days later to clean out joint debris, typically a situation that would require several weeks of recovery time and prevent him from participating in the postseason. Dr. Don Roberts, the team physician, again performed the needed medical procedure. Roy was a reluctant spectator as the Trail Blazers took on the Phoenix Suns in the opening round of the playoffs without him, his team gamely pulling an upset in the opener in Arizona before losing badly in consecutive games.

Eight days after surgery, Roy shocked everyone with what came next. Surprisingly, he was cleared to play again and was inserted into Game Four at the Rose Garden, exciting Trail Blazers fans and leaving TV analysts shaking their heads. The night before, Roy text-messaged Nate McMillan, imploring the Portland coach to let him play. He didn't say it, but Roy might have felt obligated to be on the floor after receiving that big contract. He admitted only to feeling some guilt in sitting in the training room rather than being on the floor. Allen and Pritchard, the owner and general manager, had to sign off on Roy's early return request. Wearing a black rubberized sleeve on his right knee, Roy was cheered enthusiastically when he came out for warm-ups and received a rousing standing ovation when he entered the game in the first quarter. McMillan said he felt chills when Roy went to the scorer's table.

Similar to when he injured his hamstring, Roy again appeared stiff and tentative as he moved up and down the floor. Yet he did a halftime interview with TNT sideline reporter Craig Sager, telling everyone he had been shooting all week and felt fine, that he was just a little out of shape. Roy was applauded for his toughness, but his team was assailed again for taking a chance with his health. "You just wonder what the Portland Trail Blazers were thinking," Charles Barkley said bluntly on TNT's halftime show from Atlanta. "He's the franchise. He's the whole show. I don't know if I'd take that chance."

Roy proved sturdy enough, delivering ten points, including a late three-pointer, that swung momentum Portland's way, and the Trail Blazers went on to a 96-87 victory to even the series. It was a momentary adrenaline rush for him and his team, which would be eliminated from the postseason by the Suns in six games. Roy scored five and fourteen points in the ensuing losses and later admitted his legs didn't have much bounce, certainly nothing close to the springiness he had enjoyed in his fifty-two-point game against the same team in December 2008. If nothing else, he found some solace in coming back and finishing the season with his teammates.

While he missed out on ultimate rewards, reluctantly forced to skip the All-Star Game and miss three playoff games, Roy's fourth season was another success. He consistently played at an elite level whenever strong and healthy. Although limited to sixty-five regular-season games because of his hamstring and knee setbacks, he averaged 21.5 points, 4.4 rebounds, and 4.7 assists per game, numbers that were much greater before the injuries, while the shorthanded Trail Blazers somehow compiled a 50-32 record in the regular season and advanced to the playoffs for the second consecutive year. Keep Roy and this team healthy, and there's no telling what could happen.

Roy was this devoted family man, a fan favorite, and highly a decorated player. Marketing seemed like a natural next step. For endorsements, Roy lent his name to energy drink Muscle Milk, AT&T cellular phones, an NBA video game, Wrigley's gum, and Nike products. In promoting them as the league's young guns, Nike convinced Utah's Deron Williams, Memphis's Rudy Gay, and Roy each to have a basketball-shoe line that would be sold only in their respective playing regions. The shoes, however, proved so popular that Nike sold them everywhere. Roy had a black-and-red shoe for public consumption, and an all-red shoe released only in limited edition and to family members, with each shoe sporting a BR7 logo.

Could this have been the start of a major marketing campaign that crossed all cultural lines and made Roy a household name and bigger celebrity, and not just another great basketball player? The answer was no. Roy had other ideas. He expressed a desire to be in his children's lives as much as possible and not on TV during every commercial break. He created The Brandon Roy Foundation, where he dedicated both time and money. The foundation was headquartered in Seattle and connected to similar projects in Portland. Its purpose was to fund educational needs. Specifically, it provided testing for grade school and middle school students to combat learning disorders, such as the one he struggled with that went unchecked and nearly cost him a chance to attend college.

Roy was as serious about this philanthropic effort as he was about faking Ron Artest into the air and driving around him to the basket. He promoted the foundation by building an outdoor basketball court at the intersection of Southwest Alaska Street and Delridge Way Southwest in West Seattle. There were fiberglass backboards installed on each end and a smooth surface to run on. The court was purposely designed in familiar shades of purple and white, the Garfield colors, and had Roy's and the sponsors' names painted inside a midcourt logo. If the address sounded familiar, that's because the outdoor court was built on the eastern edge of the Delridge Playfield grounds, or about two and a half blocks from the Roy family's former rental home.

"I don't want to just sell sneakers, though it's okay if kids buy mine," Roy said without any pretense or outside influence as he explained his involvement. "I want to sell kids on education. I want to be a role model in other ways. I want them to know what I stand for, and it's not just basketball."

Tiger Woods made similar promises about image when he played his way to golf championship after championship, posed in front of luxury cars, and promoted Nike athletic equipment shamelessly, before his double life filled with infidelity was revealed and ridiculed, exposing him as a fraud. Yet while Woods was sneaking off to Las Vegas and arranging sordid meetings with high-priced call girls, Roy remained a hard person to pry from his suburban home. Roy was more inclined to plant a big kiss on his son B. J.'s cheek than that of some fantasy-world stranger. Forever demonstrating a disdain for driving, even with expensive vehicles in the driveway, Roy was more apt to slide into the passenger's seat when Tiana picked him up after practice and carted him home to his uncomplicated world.

Roy had strayed from convention only in the fact that he was the father of two young children, Brandon Jr. and Mariah, before he was married. He was always open to a wedding ceremony, but said the demands of his whirlwind NBA lifestyle—long seasons, surgeries, endorsements, and contract negotiations—created inescapable delays. Brandon and Tiana, boyfriend and girlfriend since he was a junior and she was a freshman at Seattle's Garfield High, had wanted to get married during the summer of 2009. He had given her an engagement ring that was hidden in an upstairs drawer at home, but his second salary negotiations went into overtime before a settlement was reached, postponing everything of a personal nature. The couple's commitment never wavered.

On September 4, 2010, Brandon and Tiana wed in their backyard. It was a simple yet stylish ceremony. Only 210 people were invited. The guest list was largely devoid of pro basketball players, with just then-Atlanta Hawks guard Jamal Crawford, Memphis Grizzlies forward and former Blazers teammate Zach Randolph, and former NBA guard and China-bound Will Conroy present. University of Washington coach Lorenzo Romar joined them.

A private security force worked inside the gates and a police presence was stationed outside, keeping wedding crashers away. People needed a pass to get on the grounds. They needed another pass to enter the house. The wedding was a scaled-down version of what was previously planned and canceled earlier in the summer; there were fears of holding an opulent wedding ceremony while the rest of the country was still coming out of a recession. This was an agreeable alternative.

Brandon, in a black tuxedo, and Tiana, in a white dress, made the long walk across their backyard and down a sloping path to a gazebo constructed for the occasion and decorated in chiffon. The minister was Tiana's uncle, and he addressed the couple while standing below and looking up at them. Biblical verses were recited. Brandon, when asked for his marital vow of fidelity with multiple questions, responded, "I do, I shall, I will." A comedic moment came when Brandon, ready to kiss the bride, looked perplexed when he stood there for the longest time, waiting for the minister to make the request. Brandon couldn't get the attention of his minister, who momentarily had looked away.

As for a honeymoon, the newly married Brandon and Tiana Roy also kept things simple. They spent the week in their Tualatin home after shipping the kids to their grandparents' house in Renton. "We're homebodies," Tiana said. "We just relaxed for a week, because Brandon travels so much and I'm scared to death to fly."

After officially cementing his relationship with Tiana, it was time for Brandon to play basketball again. Training camp was just a month away. The Trail Blazers had a lot invested in Roy, monetarily and emotionally. They hoped he would lead them to another NBA championship, matching the Bill Walton-inspired title run of the 1976-77 season. The large gold trophy from the franchise's ultimate moment of glory was displayed in a thick glass case in the lobby of the Trail Blazers' practice facility in south Portland, serving as an everyday reminder for the next generations of players passing through the building. It wasn't hard to see the connection front-office people had tried to make between the Trail Blazers' glorious past and their promising future, with the guard from Garfield High School in the middle of this timeline. For the 2009-10 season, sharing the team entryway with the championship trophy were eight large game photos, framed and hung on two walls. Five of the images were of Roy shooting, blocking, and celebrating.

Facing college basketball limbo, Roy once thought he might never be heard from again. Now practically everyone in Portland had designated Roy as one of the city's sacred institutions. The pros lost interest in him when he injured his knee in college, but came to praise and pay him over and over. His original AAU basketball team once didn't see him as anything but a deep sub and damaged goods. His high school coach didn't readily see a professional player. His NBA team didn't see a multiple All-Star player.

"We had such high expectations, but he's surpassed that so much," Pritchard said. "He's been incredible with the way he can take a team and put it on his back, especially in the fourth quarter. I thought he could do it. I [just] didn't think he could do it at this level. I'd be lying if I said that."

Chapter 17

Deep Knee Bends

Entering his fifth season in the NBA, Brandon Roy had his world in order. He was newly married. He was in the first year of a five-year, $83 million contract. He was more popular in Portland than ever, further endearing himself to his fans the previous April by playing in the postseason just eight days after having arthroscopic knee surgery, showing himself willing to do whatever was necessary even it meant risking his fragile health.

Yet if there was an unwelcome pattern to Roy's basketball existence, it was this: The good times never lasted long. There was always some unforeseen challenge lurking around the corner. For whatever reason, Roy periodically had to suffer some sort of hardship, be humbled, and demonstrate all over again how strong he was in the face of adversity. He had struggled with his grades as a teenager, putting his college scholarship in doubt and sending him to that waterfront container yard while all of his basketball peers were headed to practice and class. He repeatedly had to prove to everyone how good he could be at every level of basketball, from middle school to college to the NBA, temporarily held out of lineups or omitted from All-America teams in college and mock draft lottery positions before people finally wised up. And, at every step, those troublesome knees got in the way.

Roy didn't have to be reminded that, as an eighth-grader, he sat out an entire basketball season because both knees ached from tendinitis. The summer before his high school senior year, with college recruiters closely monitoring his progress, he tore meniscus in his left knee and had arthroscopic surgery. Off to a sensational start as a college junior, he tore meniscus in his right knee and required more arthroscopic surgery. Early on at the professional level, he submitted to arthroscopic surgery once more on each knee, including the procedure on his right knee that led to that premature playoff return. He made a lot of comebacks.

"It's the message I always give to kids," Roy said. "They always said, 'Brandon Roy is a better person than a basketball player,' and I've been an All-Star, and that says a lot to me that people would say that. I tell kids to be a better person than a player."

Roy's knees admittedly felt sluggish during training camp, which was something new for him and caused him to sit out more workouts than usual, yet the 2010-11 NBA season began promising enough. He helped the Trail Blazers win their first three games, scoring twenty-four, twenty-two, and twenty-nine points in the process. There was no reason to think his fifth year in the league wouldn't be as sensational as the first four. He was his same game-changing self early on. Yet eight contests into the schedule—which included a taxing stretch of four road games over seven nights—Roy came up lame. Against the Los Angeles Lakers, he looked like he was running in mud. He resembled a luxury car with a couple of flat tires. It all happened so quickly that people weren't sure what to make of it at first. In a 121-96 blowout loss at the Staples Center, Roy attempted just six shots and scored only eight points, and afterward everyone from Lakers superstar Kobe Bryant to the probing Portland beat writers noted how Roy didn't look right on the floor. He played three more games and continued to struggle, finally pulling himself and limping off the court midway through a twenty-point loss in New Orleans. His left knee hurt, he finally admitted. He would sit out the next three games.

Roy would go through a month of pure basketball hell. He had swelling and stiffness in his left knee. He had it drained of fluid twice. He took anti-inflammatory medication. He took injections of Orthovisc, which acted as a lubricant. He did strengthening exercises. He submitted to magnetic resonance imaging, a medical procedure known commonly as an MRI, for visual documentation of his troubles. He was examined thoroughly by Dr. Don Roberts, the team physician who now knew Roy's knees on an intimate basis. The Trail Blazers approached a Los Angeles specialist, Dr. Neal El Attrache, for a second opinion. Roy had quit playing in New Orleans because he felt a sharper pain than he was accustomed pierce through that problematic left knee. He next admitted that neither knee held any meniscus, the sponge-like material that serves as a shock absorber, and he was playing with bone rubbing on bone in both joints. He talked of limiting his game-night minutes to ease the discomfort.

Roy returned for twelve more Trail Blazers games, and he continued to struggle. From one of the NBA's most effective penetrators, he had now become a spot-up shooter, neutralized and compromised as the special player he once was. There were limited moments of success, with his twenty-six-point effort in a 104-94 victory at Phoenix hailed as his closest return to form yet done on sheer grit alone. He followed up that effort with subpar games of nine, seven, and four points in consecutive losses at San Antonio, Memphis, and Dallas, collectively hitting just nine of thirty-seven shots. After the game in Tennessee, Roy's frustration bubbled over when he suggested that Portland's lack of outside shooters were limiting his opportunities—reporters presumed that headstrong point guard Andre Miller was a convenient scapegoat here—and Roy quickly realized what he had done and backtracked with public and private apologies. It was his sore knees talking, nothing more, and he realized it.

Things came to a head on December 15, 2010, when Roy was ineffective in the game against the Mavericks, and concerned Portland officials shut him down indefinitely. Roy acknowledged that his right knee had now become a bigger problem than the left one, presumably because he had been forced to favor the healthier knee. He could handle the pain in his left knee, but not in his right one, too. The initial plan was to rest him for an undetermined amount of time. One week turned into two. Two turned into three. There was talk he might miss the rest of the season. There were no easy answers or solutions.

Not playing well, or not playing at all, was hard enough for Roy. Now there was rampant second-guessing and intense speculation surrounding the fallen superstar. One suggestion was Roy's basketball career was over.

Or that he would be discarded by the Trail Blazers in a trade. Or that he would accept a reserve role on a permanent basis.

"The whole trip was disappointing," Roy said. "I was mentally upset that things had changed for me physically. There really was no answer. I hit a low point after the Dallas Mavericks game. I was down. I'd been playing with one knee with a lot of wear and tear, and I hadn't had a significant tear until I tore the right one against the Lakers [in April]. Now I had to learn how to play on two knees that were pretty much bone on bone, and it was an adjustment for me. I was learning how to play with another obstacle in my life."

Trail Blazers fans could be excused for contemplating the worst. They had watched Greg Oden, the former NBA No. 1 draftee and their supposed center of the future, become injured nonstop once joining the franchise, and ultimately have invasive microfracture knee surgery that season that rendered him unavailable for the second consecutive year. Longtime Portland fans had witnessed Bill Walton, another overall No. 1 draft pick and the projected face of the franchise, fall apart physically in dramatic and agonizing fashion. Walton led the Blazers to their only NBA championship in 1977, but he lasted just five seasons in Portland before foot and ankle injuries curtailed his career and transformed the former UCLA center into a journeyman player roaming the league.

As for Roy, those closest to him came to his defense, asking for patience, reminding people that adversity had always been part of his basketball career, and that he had always been able to bounce back. This knee thing wasn't anything new for him, though the pain might have been at a greater level than he previously absorbed. Roy was still a survivor, a battler, someone who seemingly could beat the odds.

"I've been knowing B-Roy since the fifth grade, and the one thing I know about him is he's a real positive guy, and I know B-Roy will never give up," old friend and fellow NBA guard Nate Robinson said. "He's a fighter, man, and he loves the game of basketball and he'll bounce back and he'll be all right."

"Everybody is writing him off," Blazers coach Nate McMillan told reporters while his best player sat injured and idle. "They're saying that he should retire or that we should move on. Well, I'm not ready to do that." Trail Blazers president Larry Miller acknowledged to the *Oregonian* that the fragility of Roy's knees was raised during their previous contract discussions, but the franchise had been willing to take that $83 million gamble on the guard's health because his pristine image meant so much to the organization. Miller described Roy's knees as an acute problem rather than a chronic problem, and expressed confidence that his All-Star guard could still maintain a high level of productivity, even if the guard had to change his playing style some. Miller used Michael Jordan as an example, explaining how Jordan had altered his game as he grew older and past his prime, and was effective.

Still, Roy showed up at 11 p.m. on Christmas Eve at the Blazers' training center and found only team employee Steve Gordon inside the facility. Roy admitted that he wasn't sure he could play anymore, bringing Gordon to tears. "That was just a brutal moment," Gordon said. "I took it way worse than he did."

After more than a month on the sidelines, Roy underwent more arthroscopic surgery on January 17, 2011, in Vancouver, Washington—on both knees. It was his fifth and sixth procedures. If that wasn't distressing enough, three days earlier, he had to drive to Seattle to attend the funeral for one of his aunts, Joyce Roy, who had died suddenly from an intestinal illness. He received the news of her passing after taking a red-eye flight back to Portland from San Francisco, where he had traveled for yet another medical opinion on his knees. At the memorial service, he saw his grandmother, Frances Roy, always the strong one, turn sad again and that was as difficult for him to comprehend as an adult as it was as a child. Yet this trip back to his hometown was cathartic in a lot of ways.

"I've always had to put basketball before family, and that's always been difficult for me, but the grieving was actually good for me," Roy said. "I got to be around my cousins who needed me. I had to be there for them. I was just so happy to be back with my family. I didn't think about my knees. I was really ready to have surgery because of my auntie. That was a tough process there, but I thought that was a moment that put things in perspective."

Two and a half weeks later, Roy eased back into practice with the Trail Blazers at the Tualatin practice site. He insisted his right knee no longer had pain while his left one still carried some discomfort, which was a promising development. He wanted to play in a Trail Blazers game right away. He said he felt strong and well rested. Yet the team had to dull his enthusiasm, asking Roy to be patient in the days ahead, to slow down and wait until the timing was right for his return, and he didn't argue. The Blazers wanted him to wait until after the All-Star break, which he used to return to Seattle and surround himself with family members once again.

"I think the pressure came off me because now there was no pressure on me," Roy said. "It was just go out and do what I always do. I was not going to be the Brandon Roy like last year, but every year I've adjusted my game some way. It's how can I get better? Let's do something and move on."

Roy played in twenty-six more regular-season games, plus six playoff games against the Dallas Mavericks, all as a reserve, but he was a shadow of his former self. He scored in double figures just nine times, and more than twenty points just twice. He averaged only eighteen minutes of playing time per game. People around the NBA whispered a little more loudly that his basketball career appeared finished. If he knew the end was near at that time, Roy wasn't ready to walk away without offering one more glimpse of his greatness. However, he had to suffer again before he could celebrate.

The Trail Blazers dropped their first two playoff games in Dallas, and Roy provided two and zero points. In Game Two, a 102-89 loss, each of the Blazers starters played thirty-five minutes or more, while Roy was limited to fewer than eight minutes, and he was clearly upset by it. When asked about his greatly reduced role, Roy told reporters he had felt like crying on the bench and was profoundly disappointed by the snub. Some fans lashed out at him for his candor; fifty-six percent responding to an *Oregonian* poll said Roy didn't deserve any more game minutes than he received. "Going from being an All-Star to the third guy off the bench was tough," he said. He was at rock bottom as an NBA player.

However, two days later in Portland, Roy was far more engaged with the Trail Blazers, playing twenty-three minutes and scoring sixteen points in a 97-92 victory over the Mavericks. It was a nice bounce-back. It was a warm-up. It was a reprieve. All the hard feelings were momentarily forgotten. A career moment was coming.

In Game Four, Roy reached down deep for an incredible performance. For twenty-four minutes, he played like an All-Star again. In an unforgettable Saturday matinee showing against Dallas, he relied on his trademark crossover dribble and attacked the basket again, something that had been lost following the latest round of knee surgeries. He had everyone at the Rose Garden standing and cheering wildly for him. He scored eighteen of his twenty-four points in the fourth quarter to lead the Trail Blazers to an 84-82 victory, rescuing them from a mammoth twenty-three-point deficit—and enabling his team to make one of the greatest comebacks in NBA playoff history.

Roy had felt chills before when he had done great things on the basketball floor, but never for such a long period of time. In Game Four, he felt those telltale chills rage through his body for the entire fourth quarter. He also was as mad as he can get.

Used sparingly again in the opening half, Brandon took the floor in the third quarter with his team way behind and a Portland fan yelled out, "God damn Roy, you aren't doing shit!" Roy heard it and seethed. He had barely played and he couldn't believe this guy was blaming him for the huge deficit. He was really angry with this faceless but acid-tongued Blazers follower. Roy silently muttered an expletive and told himself "to just play." He had a shot rattle in and he was on his way. He was as stunned as anyone when shot after shot continued to drop, even shots that didn't feel right when they came off his hand. Roy called it the best thirteen or fourteen minutes of basketball that he ever played. His emotions had swung wildly, but his play had been steady as ever. "I've never been so mad and locked in," he said.

The magic was welcome but only temporary. The Blazers' season ended with two ensuing losses, sending Dallas on its way to the NBA championship and Roy into an unwanted offseason purgatory. A sense of finality hung over this postseason rollercoaster ride.

Chapter 18

The Comeback

The NBA went on strike, locking out the players and wiping out a month and a half of games on the 2011-12 schedule. An exhaustive settlement brought everyone rushing back to play—except Brandon Roy. On December 9, 2011, two weeks before the season's designated restart, the Trail Blazers made the stunning announcement that their veteran guard had retired because of his deteriorating knees.

In a prepared statement, Roy was quoted as saying he had followed Dr. Don Roberts' advice and chosen not to risk permanent injury. That wasn't quite the case. Portland had exercised the newly negotiated amnesty clause, enabling the franchise to dump one player's contract from salary-cap considerations, in this case Roy's remaining $68 million, and the Trail Blazers were told by Brandon to handle the details of his departure however they wished. The team came up with a somewhat creative explanation for Roy's exit, not wishing to enrage the loyal Portland fan base by telling it that the team's most popular player had been unceremoniously sent on his way.

"I never retired," Roy said. "I gave them the option out of respect for them. They had done things out of respect for me. They chose the medical retirement route. It cleared the salary cap to sign Jamal [Crawford]. I never wanted to say I was retired. I just wasn't playing. That was a weird time. I thought I was going to be in Portland ten to twelve years. I thought that was the only place I'd be."

For months Roy had kept a low profile, working out in solitude. His knees admittedly felt worse than ever. They didn't recover like before. He could hear a clicking sound inside. Still, he was willing to press on, thinking the Blazers might trade him, and his knees would settle down to the point he could play at a respectable level again. Instead, he was dropped for financial reasons. He had seen this coming, warned by his agent that Portland was leaning toward using the amnesty clause on him. Still, it hurt when it happened.

"For the first time in my life, I felt a team didn't want me," Roy said. "I felt like I got cut. I wouldn't say I was a failure, but it was like a team didn't want me. I could have protested and said I was going to play, but they still would have amnestied me. I didn't protest, because I wasn't really wanted there anymore."

Roy had appeared in 336 Trail Blazers games, including the playoffs, and scored 1,107 points, averaging nineteen per game, and done a lot of stuff in a maddeningly short amount of time. Now it was over, or at least the Portland portion of his career was done. He involuntarily became a former pro basketball player at age twenty-seven.

In a harried and highly emotional disconnect, Roy had met with the Trail Blazers' doctor and received his diagnosis on a Thursday, watched the team prepare and announce his "retirement" on a Friday, and climbed in his vehicle and abandoned his handsome suburban home on Saturday, unwilling to spend another night there.

As Roy drove up Interstate 5 and headed for the comfort of Seattle, he took a call from one of Portland owner Paul Allen's representatives informing him that Allen wanted to speak to him after finishing lunch. On a speaker phone as he raced up the freeway, Brandon talked to Allen for thirty minutes. The owner offered his gratitude to Roy and made him a standing offer to return as a coach or front-office employee for the Trail Blazers if he desired. Allen asked if Roy intended to play again, and Brandon told him that he wasn't sure, but he wasn't going to take part in the upcoming season. Brandon expressed his appreciation to this powerful man for giving him the chance to become wealthy beyond his dreams.

"I thanked him for changing my kids' lives," Roy said. "He changed a lot of other kids' lives [through Brandon's foundation]. He changed my parents' lives."

Holed up in a suburban Seattle rental house not far from the Seahawks practice facility, Roy went into seclusion. For two months, he felt sorry for himself. He watched college basketball games on TV, and tried to ignore NBA telecasts, though not always successfully. He hung out with his kids, who didn't know anything different had taken place in dad's world. He mulled his future and considered coaching. He and his wife bought another house on a golf course in suburban Newcastle and put their Oregon home on the market. He spoke regularly with Crawford, his good friend and Trail Blazers roster replacement. Roy also started playing casual pick-up ball with friends and cousins at Garfield High, paying a janitor each night to let them in after 8 p.m. for a couple of hours, Monday through Thursday.

Roy resisted all attempts to get him to attend a Trail Blazers' game until he was invited down to celebrate Crawford's March 20th birthday, declined the offer, and then decided to come at the last minute and surprise his buddy. When Roy and his wife walked into the Rose Garden that night, the fans saw them on the big video screen overhead and started chanting his name, rekindling good memories.

"Blazer fans were very special," Roy said. "They played a big part in my success. I'm not better than a lot of people, but they gave me the belief that I was, like when I was going one-on-one with Kobe. They supported me through everything. When I was leaving, I thought the next time I come here it will be as a visiting player."

His comeback started like this: Will Conroy called and asked Roy to help him put former Garfield High and UW guard Tony Wroten through workouts in preparation for the NBA draft. Brandon soon was participating in all of the drills himself, doing a little more each day. Roy called Steve Gordon, the former Trail Blazers special assistant now employed by the Timberwolves, told him he felt like playing again, and they met for training sessions at a secluded Emerald City Basketball Academy gym in suburban Redmond. Conroy provided nonstop encouragement and implored his friend to keep going. It wasn't hard for Roy to say yes. He looked good. His knees didn't swell. There were no setbacks. Roy and Conroy next played five-on-five games involving former Washington teammates at suburban Renton High School. Roy dropped a few pounds and gradually got into basketball shape again.

"We were going to push him to see what he had left," Conroy said. "Every day he got better. He got to be the best guy in the gym again."

Roy's current agent, Greg Lawrence, recommended he undergo blood platelet therapy treatments as an added precaution. A couple of other agency clients, baseball players who Lawrence didn't name, had experienced success with this. Kobe Bryant and baseball player Alex Rodriguez previously had sought out this procedure in Germany, and it seemed to revitalize their careers. Roy handed over MRI photos of his well-worn knees to a doctor in California to study, and asked if there realistically was any hope for him. The doctor told Roy he was a good candidate for the therapy and he wouldn't waste his time if that wasn't the case.

In June, Roy traveled to Los Angeles for a six-day stay, accompanied by his family. They treated it like a vacation, even visiting Disneyland one afternoon. At Lifespan Medicine on Wilshire Boulevard, Roy had his blood drawn and put through a spinning process, and for five consecutive days he had this recycled blood injected into each of his knees. The procedure lasted ten minutes. Within an hour of the first shot, he noticed an improvement.

"My flexibility changed like that; I'd go work out after the shots," Roy said. In this case, an invigorated Roy headed to Loyola Marymount University for training sessions with Bill Bayno, who had been a Portland assistant coach and now worked in a similar capacity for the Timberwolves.

Creating an instant buzz, Roy went home and announced via Conroy's Twitter account that his NBA comeback was seriously under way. Roy stepped up his workouts, moving to Rainier Vista Girls and Boys Club, where his Trail Blazers jersey hung on the wall in a frame. Roy played in Crawford's Pro-Am league in the south Seattle gym, pulling on a uniform for the first time in fifteen months, ironically red and black and reminiscent of the Trail Blazers. Proving he still had star power, a group of professional autograph hunters waited nearly two hours for him to finish a long media interview session after the game, and they surrounded him in the parking lot, thrusting photos and cards at him to sign.

Six NBA teams pursued Roy's services, with the Timberwolves making the strongest push and getting him signed to a two-year, $10.4 million deal at mid-summer, with the first year guaranteed and the second granting Minnesota an injury waiver. Forty percent of that salary would go back to Portland, preventing him from double-dipping in full on two contracts, a stipulation that was part of the league's new work agreement. The Trail Blazers still were on the hook for the full amount of his $83 million contract removed from salary-cap consideration, obligated to pay it over the designated five years of the deal.

Minnesota owner Glen Taylor, president of basketball operations David Kahn, coach Rick Adelman, and trainer Gregg Farnam flew on a private jet to Seattle to meet with Roy, collectively showing so much interest in him that he couldn't help but be impressed. Roy also chose the Timberwolves over the other teams because they offered him the best opportunity to reclaim significant playing time, if not a starting job, and they required the least amount of obstacles for him to overcome to prove he was healthy again. Finally, Roy knew Bayno and the curmudgeon-like Gordon from his Portland days, and he trusted them, helping seal the connection.

"My goal was to go to the best situation," Roy said. "Contract-wise, I was happy. It had to be good enough to work. I wanted to go with a young group of guys right on the cusp to take the next step. I didn't just want to be the seventh or eighth guy. I wanted a chance to start. I thought I could fit really good with Minnesota."

In choosing the Timberwolves, Roy had to turn down an offer from Myers and the Warriors, which was a difficult task. Myers was still a good friend. Myers had been a dependable agent. They had talked throughout Roy's idle season, discussing players, games, and strategy. They regularly teased each other.

"You sure you don't want to play?" Myers asked persistently. "You could play for us."

When Roy questioned him about a game that had gotten away from Golden State in the fourth quarter, the general manager responded, "We don't have a closer. We need you."

Finally, Myers wished Roy well on his decision to play for the Timberwolves, but not without a subtle dig, saying, "I think that's a good fit for you—as long as you can handle the cold."

Once in Minneapolis, Roy posed for photos holding up jersey No. 3, choosing to wear his college digit. Derrick Williams wore No. 7 for the Timberwolves, Roy's number in Portland, and offered it to his new teammate. Roy wanted a fresh start all the way around. Three would be his new identity. The Trail Blazers' chapter of his life was officially over.

As part of his Minnesota deal, Roy arranged for the well-traveled Conroy to receive a Timberwolves' training-camp invitation and full consideration for a roster spot, facilitating yet another comeback attempt. He always took care of those around him.

Roy sounded overly optimistic about his chances of playing at a high level of pro basketball again, though he understood why everyone else preferred a wait-and-see approach. "My whole life has been like this," he said.

As he wandered easily through the Rainier Vista Girls and Boys Club, a place where basketball dreams were built, or, in his case, rekindled and restored, Roy promised that he would surprise everyone with his NBA return but he wouldn't surprise himself. He wanted to play five more years if possible. You wanted to believe him. He wanted to start again. You hoped it would happen.

EPILOGUE

Six years after hearing Minnesota call out his name on draft night, after he gladly pulled on the team's light blue hat and smiled for the cameras, and after he next learned he had been traded away to Portland in a pre-arranged deal and it was all for naught, Brandon Roy joined the Timberwolves franchise for real for the 2012-13 season.

Plenty of basketball analysts wondered whether his well-worn knees would hold up and how much game he actually had left after sitting out the season before, but people seemed genuinely pleased that Roy was back. Players such as LeBron James privately said that Brandon's knees would be protected, that there wouldn't be anyone taking cheap shots at a player of his stature, and that everyone would do their best to keep this likeable guy in the league. Fans were asked in polls which player they most wanted to see make a successful NBA comeback, and Brandon was a runaway winner.

To no one's surprise, Brandon endeared himself right away to his Midwestern setting. Reporters asked him about his early arrival for training camp. Roy could have provided the pat answer of being overanxious to get started in putting his Timberwolves career in motion, which was true. Brandon the family man was his typical honest self: He had to get his son enrolled in kindergarten.

Brandon's training camp went cautiously well and he was the only Timberwolves player to start all seven exhibition games. However, he bumped his right knee against an opposing player late in the preseason, bumped it again in the 2012-13 regular season, and Brandon lasted just five games before he was forced to the sideline. He submitted to yet another arthroscopic procedure to ease swelling, his seventh surgery dating back to high school, and he considered NBA retirement on the spot.

It wasn't clear how much longer Brandon could put up with arthritic knees that resembled faulty brakes -- his bone-on-bone discomfort was akin to a vehicle's metal-on-metal grinding, with replacement parts not reality. Explaining the wear and tear, Roy told a Portland reporter he was one step from knee-replacement surgery. For certain he had become that hard-luck elite athlete on the order of the NFL's Gale Sayers, MLB's Tony Conigliaro and NBA's Bill Walton, someone who had tasted superstardom only to have injury greatly dim his talent level after a very short time on top.

Brandon Roy had shown himself to be an exceptional NBA player, someone who could turn around a franchise, command one of the league's richest contracts, and rally an entire city around him. If only those balky knees hadn't made him mortal again.

INDEX

About the Author

A Seattle native and graduate of Western Washington University, Dan Raley was employed as a homepage editor for MSN.com after working at the *Skagit Valley Herald* in Mount Vernon, Washington; the *Fairbanks Daily News-Miner* in Alaska, *Seattle Post-Intelligencer*, and *Atlanta Journal-Constitution*.

Raley is an award-winning writer and the author of *Tideflats to Tomorrow: The History of Seattle's Sodo* and *Pitchers of Beer: The Story of the Seattle Rainiers*. His writings also have appeared in Athlon magazines, *Golf Magazine*, *Golf World*, *Golf Journal*, *Travel* and *Leisure* magazines, and the *Wall Street Journal*.

The author resides with his wife and two daughters in North Bend, Washington.